# ACKNOWLEDGMENTS

We owe special thanks to Don Morrow for visiting the Keys wildlife viewing sites, and editing the copy for many others, and to Brian Millsap of the Florida Game and Fresh Water Fish Commission for unswerving commitment to the production of this book. The following members of our committee of sponsors provided important guidance during the year this book was written: Jim Stevenson, Florida Department of Environmental Protection; Robin Will, U.S. Fish and Wildlife Service; Wendy Hale, Florida Audubon Society; Gary Evink, Florida Department of Transportation; Laurie Macdonald, Florida Chapter of the Sierra Club; Jim Karels, Department of Agriculture and Consumer Services, Division of Forestry; Dean Beyer and Don Bethancourt, U.S. Forest Service; Dr. Kathleen Shea Abrams, Department of Education; Mark Duda, Responsive Management, Inc.; Carolyn Pait, Florida Electric Coordinating Group; David Voigts, Florida Power Corporation, and Cindy Bear. Jono Miller and Julie Morris offered moral support and creative suggestions, visited many sites with us, and double-checked southwest Florida entries for accuracy.

Additional assistance came from Dr. Allan Egbert, Vic Heller, Judy Gillan, Jim Cox, Jeff Gore, Frank Smith, David Cook, Glenn Reynolds and Dave McElveen of the Florida Game and Fresh Water Fish Commission, and John Waldron, Trisha Maclaren, Dana Bryan, and Mark Glisson of the Department of Environmental Protection. Mark Robson offered invaluable logistical support and editorial assistance with south Florida sites. We are indebted to Ruth and Gordon Jerauld, Bill and Laura Nell Branan, Barbara and Eddie Hoffman, John and Swannee Nardandrea, and Jan Godown and Paolo Annino for caretaking weary travelers and offering local support.

The scope and accuracy of this book were greatly enhanced by Bill Partington, Mark Westall, Holly Tuck, Bob Repenning, Kent and Mia Van Horn, Latane Donelin, Lisa Thompson, Peggy Powell, and Barbara Samler.

Dozens of private citizens, site managers, and agency employees contributed site nominations, took us on tours, and edited parts of this manuscript. The book could not have been completed without their assistance.

We were greatly assisted by flexibility, support, and encouragement from Bram and David Canter; Don, Carson, and Anna Morrow; Jon and Susan Canter; and Martha Isleib. Our special thanks to them.

We deeply appreciate the calm guidance of Kate Davies, National Watchable Wildlife Program Manager, and John Grassy, Falcon Press editor, throughout this year.

**Author and State Project Manager:** Susan I. Cerulean
**Co-author:** Ann J. Morrow
**National Watchable Wildlife**
**Program Manager:** Kate Davies, Defenders of Wildlife
**Illustrations:** Swannee Nardandrea
**Site Maps:** Paula Ebling at Pro Image Communications
and Dana Kim-Wincapaw
**Front Cover Photo:** Roseate Spoonbill  JIM ROETZEL
**Back Cover Photo:** Female Wood Duck  JIM ROETZEL

# CONTENTS

# FLORIDA
# WILDLIFE
# VIEWING GUIDE

**Susan I. Cerulean, Author and Project Manager**
**Ann J. Morrow, Co-Author**

FALCON®

HELENA, MONTANA

*"What is there to life without the beasts?*
*And what are we without the beasts?*
*If the beasts were gone, we would die from a*
*great loneliness of spirit."*

—— Chief Seattle

This guide is dedicated to all those who would
know and protect the wildlife of Florida

# PROJECT SPONSORS

 DEFENDERS OF WILDLIFE is a national nonprofit organization of more than 200,000 members dedicated to preserving the natural abundance and diversity of wildlife and its habitat. A one-year membership is $20 and includes subscriptions to *Defenders*, an award-winning conservation magazine, and *Wildlife Advocate*, an activist-oriented newsletter. To join, or for further information, write or call Defenders of Wildlife, 1101 Fourteenth Street NW, Washington, DC 20005, (202) 682-9400. Visit their web site at http://www.defenders.org.

THE FLORIDA DEPARTMENT OF ENVIRONMENTAL PROTECTION administers Florida's state parks, aquatic preserves, and marine sanctuaries. Nearly a half million acres are managed by the Florida Park Service in 148 state parks and historic sites. State park lands are being restored to represent remnants of original natural Florida, as it appeared before Europeans arrived. Prescribed fires are used as a restoration tool, and exotic plants and animals that compete with native species are removed. State parks are open year-round for outdoor recreation, including wildlife observation. Vertebrate lists are available at many of the parks. Inquire at the park's ranger station for information on wildlife viewing. For more information, contact DEP, 3900 Commonwealth Blvd., Tallahassee, FL 32399, or call (850) 488-8666.

 THE FLORIDA DEPARTMENT OF AGRICULTURE AND CONSUMER SERVICE, DIVISION OF FORESTRY, is responsible for the protection and management of Florida's forest resources through a stewardship ethic to assure these resources will be available for future generations. The Florida Division of Forestry sponsors the Watchable Wildlife program to help promote environmental awareness and enjoyment on Florida's state forests. For further information, contact the Department of Agriculture and Consumer Services, Division of Forestry, 3125 Conner Blvd., Tallahassee, FL 32399-1650. Phone (850) 488-7616.

 FLORIDA DEPARTMENT OF TRANSPORTATION is mandated to plan, operate, and maintain a statewide multimodal transportation system. The DOT strives to provide quality engineering in an environmentally sound manner in the planning, location, design, construction, and maintenance of transportation facilities. The department recognizes that the transportation corridor is part of the total environment so that emphasis is given to preserve and enhance the existing landscape and associated wildlife through balancing engineering, environmental, and economic aspects while adhering to aesthetic design principles. For more information, contact DOT, Environmental Management Office, 605 Suwanee St., Tallahassee, FL 32399-0450. Phone (850) 922-7201.

The FOREST SERVICE, U.S. DEPARTMENT OF AGRICUL-TURE, has a mandate to protect, improve, and wisely use the nation's forest and range resources for multiple purposes to benefit all Americans. Florida's national forests, the Ocala, Osceola, and Apalachicola, containing 1,135,306 acres, are sponsors of this program to promote awareness and enjoyment of fish and wildlife on our national forest lands. For more information, contact USFS, Woodcrest Office Park, 325 John Knox Road, Suite F100, Tallahassee, FL 32303-4160. Phone (850)942-9308.

The DEPARTMENT OF DEFENSE is the steward of about 25 million acres of land in the United States, many of which possess irreplaceable natural and cultural resources. The DOD is pleased to support the Watchable Wildlife program through its Legacy Resource Management Program, a special initiative to enhance the conservation and restoration of natural and cultural resources on military land. For more information, contact the Office of the Deputy Under Secretary of Defense (Environmental Security), 400 Army Navy Drive, Suite 206, Arlington, VA 22202-2884.

THE U.S. FISH AND WILDLIFE SERVICE, DEPARTMENT OF THE INTERIOR, is proud to be a sponsor of the Florida Wildlife Viewing Guide. The agency has a mandate to conserve, protect, and enhance the nation's fish and wildlife and their habitats for the continuing benefit of the American people. The USFWS is primarily responsible for the management of migratory, freshwater and anadromous fish; protection and recovery of endangered species; enforcement of federal wildlife laws; research; and administration of the national wildlife refuge system and national fish hatcheries. U.S. Fish and Wildlife Service, Richard B. Russell Bldg., 75 Spring Street SW, Atlanta, GA 30303. Phone (404) 331-0830

THE NATIONAL FISH AND WILDLIFE FOUNDATION, chartered by Congress to stimulate private giving to conservation, is an independent nonprofit organization. Using federally-funded challenge grants, it forges partnerships between the public and private sectors to conserve the nation's fish, wildlife, and plants. National Fish and Wildlife Foundation, Bender Bldg., Suite 900, 1120 Connecticut Avenue, NW, Washington, DC 20036. (202) 857-0166.

FLORIDA ELECTRIC POWER COORDINATING GROUP, INC. (FCG) is an organization of 37 electric utilities located across the state. The goal of this alliance is to provide a reliable, adequate supply of electric power to Florida's consumers at the lowest possible cost in an environmentally sensitive manner. The FCG is pleased to sponsor this guide as part of its ongoing program of environmental stewardship, a principle firmly embedded in electric utility industry activities. For more information, write FCG, 405 Reo Street, Suite 100, Tampa, FL 33609-1004, or call (813) 289-5644.

FLORIDA POWER CORPORATION, the second-largest electric utility in the state, is sensitive to the need to protect the numerous natural areas that are found on company facilities. FPC is committed to environmental stewardship and habitat preservation so there will be wildlife for others to enjoy. For further information, contact FPC, Environmental Services, PO Box 14042, MAC H2G, St. Petersburg, FL 33733. Phone (813) 866-5166.

 The NATIONAL PARK SERVICE is charged with administering the units of the National Park System in a manner that protects and conserves their natural and cultural resources for the enjoyment of present and future generations. National Park Service, 75 Spring Street SW, Atlanta, GA 30303, (404) 331-4998.

### Other Important Contributors Include:

Florida Audubon Society • Florida Chapter of the Sierra Club
Florida Department of Education • Corkscrew Swamp Sanctuary • Archbold
Biological Station • League of Environmental Educators in Florida
Florida Wildlife Federation • Florida Defenders of the Environment

Copyright © 1998 by Falcon® Publishing, Inc., Helena, Montana.
Illustrations copyright © 1993 by Defenders of Wildlife, Washington, D.C.
Published in cooperation with Defenders of Wildlife.

4  5  6  7  8  9  10  CE  04  03  02  01  00  99

Falcon and FalconGuide are registered trademarks of Falcon® Publishing, Inc.

Defenders of Wildlife and its design are registered
trademarks of Defenders of Wildlife, Washington, D.C.

All rights reserved, including the right to reproduce this book or any part thereof in any form, except brief quotations for reviews, without the written permission of the publisher.

Design, typesetting, and other prepress work by Falcon Publishing, Helena, Montana.

Printed in Korea.
ISBN 1-56044-353-7

Cataloging-in-Publication Data

Cerulean, Susan.
    Florida wildlife viewing guide / Susan Cerulean, author and project manager, Ann J. Morrow, co-author.
        p.  cm.
    ISBN 1-56044-353-7
    1. Wildlife viewing sites—Florida—Guidebooks.  2. Wildlife watching –Florida—Guidebooks.  I. Morrow, Ann, 1952–     .
II. Defenders of Wildlife.  III. Title.  IV. Series.
QL169.C47  1993
599.09759–dc20                                                          98-18370
                                                                              CIP

Florida is a wildlife watcher's paradise! With more wildlife species than any state east of the Mississippi River, your chances of finding the viewing experience of a lifetime here are excellent. Interested in watching large flocks of herons and egrets feeding in a sea of sawgrass? You've come to the right place. A ten-foot alligator basking on the sandy bank of a crystal-clear stream? No problem. A beach and mudflat with seemingly endless flocks of shorebirds, gulls, and terns? They are here for the viewing!

What makes Florida so special? Our unique geographic position, between the temperate and tropical latitudes, provides conditions that allow both temperate and subtropical Caribbean wildlife to flourish. Couple this with a geologic history of periodic flooding by the ocean and isolation from mainland North America, and you have conditions that allowed the evolution of wild animal life found nowhere else on earth.

As the agency responsible for this rich and unique wildlife heritage, the Florida Game and Fresh Water Fish Commission is especially pleased to join with our co-sponsors in bringing you this guide. Since 1943, the Game and Fresh Water Fish Commission has managed Florida's wildlife to provide for their protection and to meet the varied demands of our citizens. Early on, the agency's primary focus was on restoring, managing, and controlling populations of game species. In 1993, as the agency celebrates its fiftieth anniversary as stewards of the state's wildlife, our role has grown and become much more diverse.

Florida's wildlife faces tremendous challenges as our state continues to grow and develop; the Game and Fresh Water Fish Commission is in the forefront of efforts to see that a broad spectrum of wildlife, including nongame, threatened and endangered species, and their habitats are adequately protected and managed. In addition, Florida's citizens are becoming increasingly interested in wildlife watching. As this book attests, we welcome this interest, and are anxious to facilitate the enjoyment of all that Florida's wildlife has to offer.

So grab your binoculars and a field guide or two, and enjoy the thrill of experiencing Florida's wildlife. No matter where you start—the shady, deep, steephead ravines in the Panhandle that support a unique mix of salamanders and frogs, the ancient sand dune ridges of central Florida that support the scrub oak communities required by the Florida scrub jay and sand skink, or the limestone- and coral-studded keys that support thriving tropical hammocks replete with Florida tree snails, white-crowned pigeons, and the diminutive key deer— you're in for an unforgettable wildlife experience. Enjoy Florida's wildlife, and help us to protect it!

Allan L. Egbert, Ph. D.

Executive Director
Florida Game and Fresh
Water Fish Commission

# TO THE READER

We are pleased to offer you this second edition of the *Florida Wildlife Viewing Guide*. We have added thirty-two new sites where you can enjoy our state's abundant and diverse natural beauty, and we have updated information about old favorites.

# INTRODUCTION

Whether your destination is the monarch butterfly migration in north Florida, or all 1.5 million acres of Everglades National Park, this book can guide you to many memorable wildlife viewing experiences. We can't guarantee exactly when you'll see a bottle-nosed dolphin, or that you'll ever see a Florida black bear, but you're sure to encounter Florida's native wildlife on their own terms, and in their native habitats. Among the continental United States, Florida has bred more species of plants and animals than any other state except California and Texas. The sites in this guide offer a wonderful sampling of the state's biodiversity.

More than 250 natural areas were considered for the Florida Wildlife Viewing Guide, and stringent standards were used to evaluate and select 96. Many worthy sites were not included due to space limitations; quite a few were eliminated to protect fragile wildlife and habitat from damage.

As you visit these sites, identification of the animals you see will be your first step, but if you watch closely, you may see them feed (on what?), clean or dry themselves, court or mate, defend territories, or make nests (with what materials, from where?). An alligator dredging a water hole will often attract a heron or egret to gobble up small fish scattered by the gator's activity. Or you may see a wasp dig a hole, fly in with a paralyzed spider, and pull it down the hole in order to feed its larvae.

As you travel, get involved in the detective work of "reading the Florida landscape." Slight elevation changes produce different plant communities and habitats. Wetlands are often only inches or a few feet below dry land, and well-drained, desertlike scrub and sandhill communities in the center of the peninsula are only a hundred feet or more above sea level. Watch for changes in these plant communities—the wildlife species will change accordingly.

Use this guide to engage your understanding and imagination of the biological richness Florida has to offer. May it also inspire you to support agencies and private organizations that are working to safeguard Florida's wildlife and wildlands legacy.

# THE NATIONAL WATCHABLE WILDLIFE PROGRAM

The Florida Watchable Wildlife Project is part of a national response to growing public interest in wildlife viewing and the need to develop new public support for wildlife conservation efforts. As part of the National Watchable Wildlife Program coordinated by Defenders of Wildlife, 15 government agencies and private organizations in Florida have joined forces and funds to promote wildlife viewing, conservation, and education. The Florida Wildlife Viewing Guide is an important first step in this effort.

This book is much more than a guide: the sites are part of a national wildlife viewing network. The partnership formed to produce the Florida guide and the network will continue to work together on site development, interpretation, and conservation education. Travel routes to each site will be marked with the brown-and-white binoculars sign appearing on the cover of this book. Travelers will also notice these signs in other states. As similar partnerships are formed in other states, the United States eventually will be linked by a network of wildlife viewing sites.

Site enhancement of individual viewing sites is the next step. This will involve such things as interpretive signs, trail development, viewing blinds or platforms, and provisions for parking and restrooms. Many sites in this guide are already developed as Watchable Wildlife areas, while others provide only access at this time.

The National Watchable Wildlife Program is founded on the notion that the surest means to create support for wildlife is to first capture the heart. To view wildlife in a natural setting—a sunset flight of sandhill cranes, a mother manatee and her calf—is to feel awe, excitement, wonder. These experiences become the foundation upon which each of us builds an appreciation for and understanding of the natural systems and diversity of wildlife that surround us. From there, a person need only take the shortest of steps to feel genuine concern for our natural heritage, and its continued protection into the future.

# HOW TO USE THIS GUIDE

This guide is divided into seven travel regions, each coded a different color for quick reference. Wildlife viewing sites are listed and located on a map at the beginning of each region. Each site includes the following elements to help describe and interpret wildlife and habitats you may see.

**Description:** This gives a brief account of the habitat and wildlife.

**Viewing Information:** This section expands on the site description and gives the seasonal likelihood of spotting wildlife at the site. It may include information about access, parking, and WARNINGS in capital letters.

**Directions:** Written descriptions are provided for most sites. If the site is slightly difficult to locate, a full-color map is provided. Roads, nearby towns, access points, and other viewing information is printed on these maps. NOTE: PLEASE SUPPLEMENT THE MAPS IN THIS GUIDE WITH AN UP-TO-DATE FLORIDA ROAD MAP. The map number provided refers to the indispensable DeLorme Florida Atlas and Gazetteer.

**Ownership:** Provides the name of the agency, organization, or company that owns or manages the site. The telephone number listed may be used to obtain more information.

**Recreation and Facility Symbols:** These indicate some of the facilities and opportunities available at each site. The managing agency can provide more information. The camping, restaurant, lodging, and boat ramp symbols mean that these facilities are available within the site boundaries.

## FACILITIES AND RECREATION

| Parking | Restrooms | Barrier-free | Lodging | Restaurant | Picnic | Camping | Fishing |

| Boat Ramp | Large Boats | Small Boats | Hiking | Bicycling | Horse Trails | Entry Fee | Hunting |

## HIGHWAY SIGNS

As you travel in Florida and other states, look for these signs on highways and other roads. They identify the route to follow to reach wildlife viewing sites.

WILDLIFE VIEWING AREA

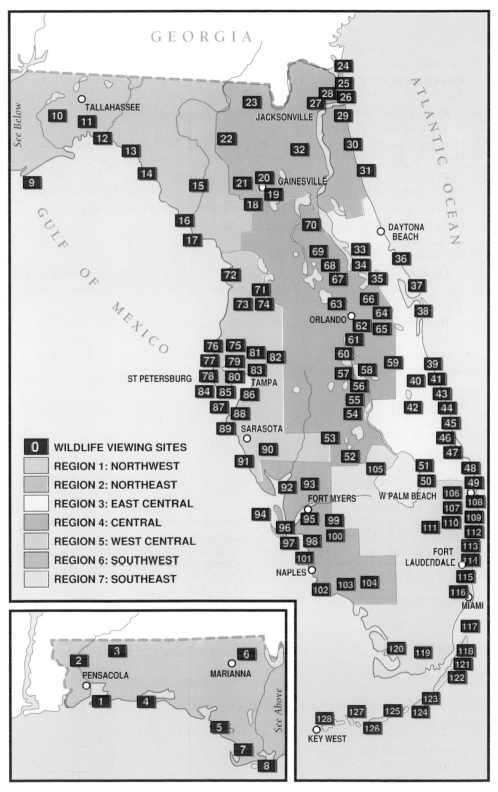

GEORGIA

ATLANTIC OCEAN

GULF OF MEXICO

See Below

TALLAHASSEE

10
11
12
13
14
9
15
16
17

23
JACKSONVILLE
24
25
28 26
27
29
30
31

22
32

21 20 GAINESVILLE
18 19

70
DAYTONA BEACH
69
68
67
33
34
35
66
64
63 65
62
61
60
57 58 59
56
55
54
36
37
38
39
40 41
43
42
44
45
46
47

72

71
73 74

76 75
77 79 81 82
78 80 83
84 85 86
87 88
89 SARASOTA
90
91

ST PETERSBURG
TAMPA

ORLANDO

53
52
105
51
50
48
49
W PALM BEACH
106
107
108
109
110
111 112
113
FORT LAUDERDALE 114
115
116 MIAMI

92 93
FORT MYERS
94
96 95 99
97 98 100
101
NAPLES
102 103 104

117
120 119 118
121
122
123
127 125 124
128 126
KEY WEST

0  WILDLIFE VIEWING SITES
REGION 1: NORTHWEST
REGION 2: NORTHEAST
REGION 3: EAST CENTRAL
REGION 4: CENTRAL
REGION 5: WEST CENTRAL
REGION 6: SOUTHWEST
REGION 7: SOUTHEAST

GEORGIA

2
PENSACOLA
3
6
MARIANNA
1
4
5
7
8

See Above

15

# BEFORE YOU GO:

Decide which animals you'd like to see. Colorful warblers? Nesting bald eagles? Manatees?

Look in the right places. Every animal lives in a particular habitat, a place that provides the combination of food, water, and cover an animal needs for nesting, hiding, feeding, and sleeping. You'll be most successful locating the animals you want to see if you know where they live. Check the species index on page 162 for good locations to start.

Find out the times of day and year your sought-after species are most viewable. Plan your trip accordingly. For example, American robins, common loons, and cedar waxwings spend only the winter months in Florida. Others, like certain hawks and many warblers, are present only during their migration through the state, from March through May, and again from September through October. If you plan to view sea turtles laying eggs, you need to plan your trip for the summer months.

During your first visit to a particular site, you may not encounter all resident and migratory wildlife. The more you visit an area, the greater your chances of spotting different species. Many animals are most active at dawn and dusk.

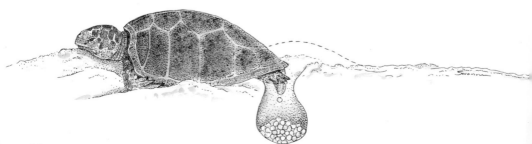

# WHAT TO TAKE:

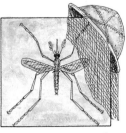

Binoculars, spotting scopes and telephoto lenses are great aids in getting close-up views of wildlife. Binoculars come in sizes

such as 7x35, 8x40, and 10x50. The smaller number refers to how large the animal will be magnified compared to the unaided eye. A "7x" means that the animal is magnified 7 times larger. A disadvantage of larger magnifications is that your hand movements will be magnified that much more. A bird in a tree will be harder to find with a 10x magnification than with a 7x, because even your breathing will cause the image to move. The larger number in the couplet refers to the diameter of the larger lens that faces the animal. The larger that number, the more light will be gathered, hence the better for viewing wildlife in dim light.

Consider your need for protective clothing for each outdoor wildlife adventure. Mosquitoes, flies, ticks, and chiggers are common Florida residents from the late spring through fall. Bring along insect repellent and a hat. Protect your skin and eyes from intense sunlight. Polarized sunglasses can help you see manatees and other aquatic animals beneath the water's surface. A canteen of water is a good idea to pack along on longer hikes. If you're not prepared, your stay will be shortened, decreasing your chances of seeing wildlife.

- ☐ Binoculars
- ☐ Spotting Scope
- ☐ Telephoto Lenses
- ☐ Sunscreen
- ☐ Hat
- ☐ Insect Repellent

# WHEN YOU ARRIVE:

There are at least three different ways to find wildlife once you arrive at the viewing area you've chosen: hide in a blind or your car and wait for animals to pass nearby; call certain species to you; or actively follow an animal by sight or tracks.

When you walk into a wildlife viewing area, the featured birds and mammals often flee as you approach. Find a comfortable place to sit, lean against a tree or bench, and relax, but be perfectly still. This is a tough technique for the impatient and restless, but if you're patient, you may be rewarded with memorable sights.

You can become actively involved in enticing wildlife to come to you. By repeating, in a rhythmic manner, the sound "psssh," which imitates scolding birds and squirrels, you can attract chickadees, nuthatches, warblers, and vireos. Remember, though, prolonged calling can harass the animal and distract it from feeding or caring for its young.

Don't forget to use your ears to identify wildlife. You may not see that frog, warbler or cricket, but if you learn the calls, you'll feel satisfied knowing the animal is nearby. Tapes of the calls of Florida birds and frogs are available for purchase.

Though Florida's wildlife is very abundant, you may, at times, miss the opportunity to observe it. Learn to read the signs or "calling cards" left behind by wild animals. Search for tracks in mud or sand, or follow well-worn trails made by routine passages of animals such as deer, rabbits, or foxes. Nibbled branches, gnawed pine cones or nuts, droppings, burrows and tunnels, and trees with cavity holes or stripped bark also give the attentive observer clues about the presence of wildlife. Though you may never spot the animal, you can learn a great deal about its behavior and preferred habitat.

Stalking wildlife usually occurs after you've spotted an animal in the distance. This technique requires the use of all your senses in order to get close without being noticed. Keep the wind in your face , walk quietly, avoid brittle leaves or sticks, and keep vegetation between you and the animal.

Some animals can best be seen or heard at night. Great horned owls hoot, barred owls query "who cooks for you, who cooks for you all?" and screech owls quaver. Bats and flying squirrels are very active after sundown. Check your porch light or street lamp for moths, June bugs, and a host of invertebrates. In the spring, listen for chuck-will's-widows, nighthawks, spring peepers, and toads. Coyotes howl at night (and can be confused with domestic dogs!), while foxes yelp. Since animals typically cannot detect red light, take along a flashlight with its lens wrapped in red cellophane. Shine the light across fields, marshes, and forests to catch the flicker of animals' "eye shine."

Some of the best wildlife viewing in Florida is done on the water. Animals are less afraid of a canoe or boat drifting by than they are of humans on foot. Some of the viewing sites in this book offer canoe rentals at on-site concessions. Use your own, or rent a canoe to travel a few of the numerous rivers, bays, creeks, and lakes in Florida for outstanding viewing opportunities. To avoid spooking a heron, a playful otter, a dolphin, or a raft of ducks, crouch low in your boat, use your paddle as a rudder and let the current guide you in for a closer look.

# ETHICS:

If you're like most wildlife watchers, you care a great deal about the animals you seek. However, even those with the most sincere concern can place wildlife or themselves at risk unless they fully appreciate the following:

It's natural to want to get as close as possible to wildlife. But for your sake, and theirs, it's best to stay on marked trails and use binoculars or zoom lenses to extend your view. Every animal has its limits

of how close you can approach before it flees. When wildlife

watchers get too close, serious problems may arise. Energy that the animal uses to escape human disturbances is no longer available for other uses, such as escaping predators, attracting a mate, migrating, or raising young. Although the animal might easily compensate the energy cost of a single short disturbance by eating more, repeated disturbances may add up to higher costs than the animal can afford, particularly in heavily-visited wildlife areas. If you observe skittish or aggressive behavior, alarm calls, or distraction displays (such as a bird exhibiting a "broken wing" or repeated circling), you are too close. Move away slowly and immediately.

Feed yourself, not the animals. Cheese puffs, candy bars, and white bread are not what nature intended as a healthy diet for wildlife. If you think feeding wildlife is harmless, think again. When wild animals become dependent on handouts, they may approach cars and risk colliding with oncoming traffic or they may lose their natural fear of humans and become aggressive and dangerous.

Wildlife belongs in the wild. Though wild babies may look help-less, rarely are they abandoned by their parents. Usually the adults are nearby, waiting until you leave before they return. The longer you stay, the longer the young go without food, and the greater the likelihood that an animal predator will spot the vulnerable little ones. If an adult animal allows you to approach, something's wrong. It may be injured, sick, or aggressive. If you are suspicious, leave the animal alone and report the case to the local site manager.

It is against Florida law for people or pets to chase, harass, molest, or otherwise maliciously harm wildlife. Your viewing trips will be more successful if you leave your pets at home. Many properties prohibit pets altogether. Call ahead for details.

# GETTING MORE HELP:

☐

**Join a tour.** A variety of private and public groups offer nature or bird tours throughout the state. Contact your local Audubon chapter, or inquire about privately- run tours or self-employed

☐ naturalists in the area you are exploring. Many state parks offer wildlife education programs.

**Ask a wildlife biologist or naturalist** at the site you are visiting for recent sightings or concentrations of wildlife. Some sites may offer checklists of birds or mammals spotted on the property. Be sure to add your interesting sightings to any logbook kept for

☐ that purpose so the next visitors are aware of recent sightings.

**Check your library, bookstore, or nature center** for field guides to the identification of Florida's wildlife. Learn what the animal looks like, where it lives, what it likes to eat, and how it behaves. See page 163 for just a few of the dozens of excellent references about wildlife in Florida.

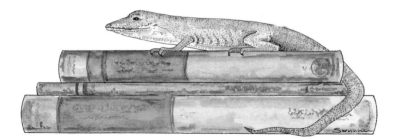

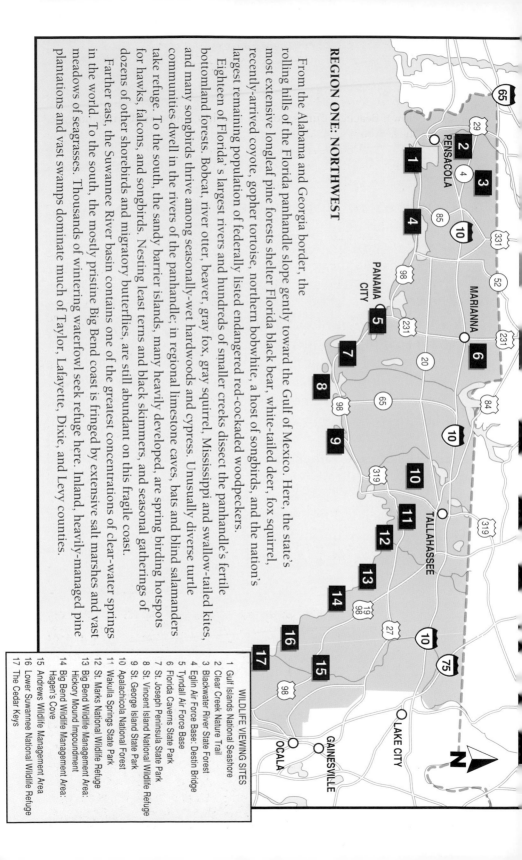

## REGION ONE: NORTHWEST

From the Alabama and Georgia border, the rolling hills of the Florida panhandle slope gently toward the Gulf of Mexico. Here, the state's most extensive longleaf pine forests shelter Florida black bear, white-tailed deer, fox squirrel, recently-arrived coyote, gopher tortoise, northern bobwhite, a host of songbirds, and the nation's largest remaining population of federally listed endangered red-cockaded woodpeckers.

Eighteen of Florida's largest rivers and hundreds of smaller creeks dissect the panhandle's fertile bottomland forests. Bobcat, river otter, beaver, gray fox, gray squirrel, Mississippi and swallow-tailed kites, and many songbirds thrive among seasonally-wet hardwoods and cypress. Unusually diverse turtle communities dwell in the rivers of the panhandle; in regional limestone caves, bats and blind salamanders take refuge. To the south, the sandy barrier islands, many heavily developed, are spring birding hotspots for hawks, falcons, and songbirds. Nesting least terns and black skimmers, and seasonal gatherings of dozens of other shorebirds and migratory butterflies, are still abundant on this fragile coast.

Farther east, the Suwannee River basin contains one of the greatest concentrations of clear-water springs in the world. To the south, the mostly pristine Big Bend coast is fringed by extensive salt marshes and vast meadows of seagrasses. Thousands of wintering waterfowl seek refuge here. Inland, heavily-managed pine plantations and vast swamps dominate much of Taylor, Lafayette, Dixie, and Levy counties.

### WILDLIFE VIEWING SITES

1 Gulf Islands National Seashore
2 Clear Creek Nature Trail
3 Blackwater River State Forest
4 Eglin Air Force Base: Destin Bridge
5 Tyndall Air Force Base
6 Florida Caverns State Park
7 St. Joseph Peninsula State Park
8 St. Vincent Island National Wildlife Refuge
9 St. George Island State Park
10 Apalachicola National Forest
11 Wakulla Springs State Park
12 St. Marks National Wildlife Refuge
13 Big Bend Wildlife Management Area: Hickory Mound Impoundment
14 Big Bend Wildlife Management Area: Hagen's Cove
15 Andrews Wildlife Management Area
16 Lower Suwannee National Wildlife Refuge
17 The Cedar Keys

# 1 GULF ISLANDS NATIONAL SEASHORE

**Description:** The Fort Pickens area of this national seashore features a historic fort and numerous concrete batteries at the western end of Santa Rosa Island (see map below). Beaches, dunes, coastal marshes, and scrubby uplands predominate. The seashore's Naval Live Oaks area is located on the mainland near Gulf Breeze. At Naval Live Oaks, the best viewing opportunities are found in the section south of U.S. Highway 98 near the visitor center. Both areas offer good birding during spring migration.

**Viewing Information:** At Fort Pickens, bottle-nosed dolphins, brown pelicans, gulls, terns, and other shorebirds are observed year-round from the beach. From the boardwalk across the dunes, look for the tracks of mice, raccoons, rabbits, and snakes. Skunks, raccoons, and opossums frequent the campground after dusk. Trail from the campground to Fort Pickens passes through brackish marshes where herons, egrets, and American bitterns forage. Look for sign of beaver activity (dams, chewings, etc.). At Naval Live Oaks, a trail from the visitor center passes through a live oak hammock featuring large magnolia, hickory, and red cedar trees. Walk along the shore of Santa Rosa Sound to view black-bellied and snowy plovers, willets, and great blue herons. Look for common loons and red-breasted mergansers in the winter. There is a nice view of the sound from the observation platform at west end of trail. Good interpretive centers at both locations. Check schedule for ranger-led walks.

*Directions: See map*
DeLorme Maps 42 and 43

**Ownership:** National Park Service (850) 934-2600
**Size:** 28,976 acres in Florida
**Closest town:** Pensacola Beach/Gulf Breeze

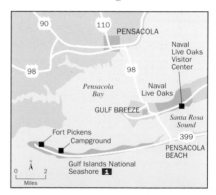

*Many visitors to Florida have seen captive Atlantic bottle-nosed dolphins performing in marine parks, but it is a real treat to observe the graceful shape of a wild dolphin breaking the surface of shallow coastal waters. Curious and playful, these mammals will sometimes follow a motorboat and "surf" in the trailing wake.*

JOHN NETHERTON

# 2 CLEAR CREEK NATURE TRAIL

**Description:** At Clear Creek, a 1.5-mile boardwalk trail winds through a variety of habitats, including sandhill uplands, botttomland hardwood, and freshwater swamp. You may want to combine this short, educational meander with a longer hike or bike through Blackwater River State Forest or State Park.

**Viewing information:** A special feature of this site is an extensive boardwalk that brings the visitor harmlessly out and over a pitcher plant bog; the spring months, April through June, are great times to see carnivorous sundews and pitcher plants in bloom. You can lie on your stomach on the boardwalk to photograph or view these plant curiosities at close range, as well as see turtles, fish, and alligators. River otters and beavers live here; you can spot beaver dams and other evidence of their construction even if you fail to see the animals themselves. The trail is within sight and sound of a military airfield which is heavily used at times. The nature trail is open daylight hours, all year.

**Directions:** From Milton, travel eight miles north on Highway 87. Turn east on Florida Highway 87A into Whiting Field. Travel one mile and turn left at the sign "Clear Creek Nature Trail"; the nature trail parking area is ahead one-half mile.

DeLorme Map 27

**Ownership:** U.S. Department of the Navy (850) 623-7181, x48
**Size:** 75 acres
**Closest town:** Milton

*The beaver's pelt was once literally worth its weight in gold. By the late 1800s, this large, heavy-bodied rodent was nearly depleted from North America. Today, it thrives in most of its former range and is found in northwest Florida, south to the mouth of the Suwannee River. Because the nocturnal beaver is difficult to see, look instead for sign of its labors—a stump or branch chewed to a point or the beaver dam itself.* JIM ROETZEL

# 3 BLACKWATER RIVER STATE FOREST

**Description:** *AUTO TOUR.* An eight-mile driving loop through longleaf pine uplands. The forest's open understory emphasizes the gently rolling terrain. The drive passes through an active colony of the federally-listed endangered red-cockaded woodpecker and close to unique pitcher plant bogs. Eastern bluebirds are plentiful. Canoeing the shallow creeks is popular.

**Viewing Information:** From Florida Highway 4, which runs east-west through the forest (see map below), turn south on Florida 191 in Munson and stop at the Blackwater Forestry Center, 0.2 mile from the intersection. Helpful maps and brochures are available here. Continue south on Florida 191 for 2.6 miles, then turn right on Spanish Trail (Forest Road 64), a hard-packed clay road. Travel 0.8 mile; on the left, look for the first of two pitcher plant bogs next to the road. Peak bloom is in April and May. *BOGS ARE FRAGILE; AVOID TRAMPLING.* Continue 2.2 miles on Spanish Trail to the stop signs at Three Notch Road (not marked). Turn left. After 0.7 mile, the road enters a red-cockaded woodpecker colony area. Active nest trees beside the road are marked with white bands and are conspicuously covered with a heavy sap flow. Drive another 1.7 miles, then turn left (east) onto paved Hardee Road and go 0.5 mile to Florida 191. The Forestry Center, open Monday through Friday (7:00 a.m. to 4:00 p.m. CST), is 5.8 miles to the north. The Florida Trail runs through the Forest.

**Directions:** *See map*
Delorme Maps 27 and 28

**Ownership:** Florida Division of Forestry (850) 957-4201
**Size:** 183,381 acres
**Closest town:** Milton

*Four types of insect-eating plants—pitcher plants, bladderworts, sundews, and butterworts—grow in wet "herb bogs" between pine flatwoods and adjoining swamps or streams.* BILL LEA

## 4 EGLIN AIR FORCE BASE: DESTIN BRIDGE

**Description:** Like other Air Force installations in Florida, Eglin shelters hundreds of thousands of acres of undisturbed wildlife habitat. The Destin Bridge site is located on a busy inlet between Okaloosa Island and the town of Destin.

**Viewing Information:** On the beaches and sandy flats, threatened least terns and snowy plovers nest and are protected from May through August. *PLEASE DON'T DISTURB; KEEP DOGS AWAY.* Other terns, gulls, black skimmers, brown pelicans, and a host of shorebird species are conspicuous much of the year. Great and little blue herons, snowy egrets, and occasionally black-necked stilts forage along the edge of the inlet and in a small interior pond. Bottle-nosed dolphins frolic year-round in the inlet. In fall, reddish egrets are sometimes seen on the sandbars in the channel. From the jetty, use a spotting scope to observe loons, northern gannets, and sea ducks offshore. Contact Eglin's Natural Resources office for an outdoor recreation map and rules summary. There are many other viewing opportunities on the base.

*Directions: From Destin, cross the bridge to Okaloosa Island on U.S. Highway 98. Parking is on left (south) side of the road.*

DeLorme Map 44

**Ownership:** U.S. Air Force (850) 882-4164
**Size:** 150 acres
**Closest town:** Destin

*The slender and elegant black-necked stilt uses its long legs to wade through six inches or more of water in search of crayfish, shrimp, snails, and tadpoles. The stilt's thin black bill, white underparts, and black wings contrast starkly with the subtler hues of Florida's shallow freshwater and saltwater habitats.*
LARRY LIPSKY

## 5 TYNDALL AIR FORCE BASE

**Description:** This active military base on a 29,000-acre peninsula adjoining the Gulf of Mexico offers wildlife observation, shelling, fishing, and swimming. Warbler's Way, a 0.25-mile elevated boardwalk with observation tower, winds through a freshwater marsh past an active wading bird rookery. One-mile Deer Run Nature Trail leads through pine flatwoods, pitcher plant bogs, and sand pine scrub. Dozens of shorebird species frequent tidal pools and beaches at the east end of the base. Ospreys are common and southern bald eagles nest along the bay.

**Viewing Information:** Two hundred pairs of herons and egrets nest from March through September in the Warbler's Way rookery. Purple gallinules and wood ducks abound. Migrating songbirds use this area heavily, especially in March and April. Deer Run Nature Trail travels through thickly populated white-tailed deer habitat. At East End Beach, black skimmers, American oystercatchers, snowy and piping plovers, and many other species are dependably present. Loggerhead sea turtles nest here on summer nights. Call the Natural Resources office to watch baby turtles hatch in late summer.

*Directions: From Panama City, travel ten miles east on U.S. Highway 98 to Tyndall Air Force Base. Drive 0.25 mile and stop at the visitor's checkpoint for a pass. Warbler's Way is 4.0 miles west on Sabre Drive on the right. To visit Deer Run, take the first left after the checkpoint and drive 0.5 mile to the natural resources building on the right. The trail begins behind the building. The access to East End Beach is one mile west of Mexico Beach on U.S. Highway 98.*

DeLorme Maps 46, 47, 59

**Ownership:** U.S. Air Force (850) 283-2641
**Size:** 29,000 acres
**Closest town:** Panama City

*Unmistakable American oystercatchers, with striking black and white coloration, heavy, bright red beaks, and pinkish legs, are uncommon residents of the Florida coast. Look for oystercatchers alone or in pairs among congregations of shorebirds, gulls and terns, especially on quiet Gulf coast beaches and islands.* JOHN GERLACH

29

**Description:** A fascinating series of caves, many with beautiful stalactites, stalagmites, and columns, delight visitors in this northern panhandle park. There are daily cave tours and miles of trails through the beech-magnolia forest and floodplain swamp bordering the Chipola River. The forest here is similar to the Appalachian foothills. The limestone outcroppings and wildflowers resemble more northern terrain. There is a significant population of bats living in certain caves (closed to the public), and the woodlands attract a variety of spring migrant birds. There is a spring for swimming, a pleasant campground, and canoeing available on the Chipola River Canoe Trail. This park is particularly busy in the summer. *SCHOOL AND TOUR GROUPS SHOULD CALL AHEAD TO RESERVE SPACE ON A GUIDED CAVE TOUR.*

**Viewing Information:** Bird species common to this floodplain forest include barred owls and red-shouldered hawks. Watch for swallow-tailed and Mississippi kites in the spring and summer, as well as vireos, flycatchers, wood thrushes, and hooded and prothonotary warblers. Ruby-throated hummingbirds are frequently seen in the spring when red, tubular flowers on columbines and buckeyes are blooming. Canoe rentals available. Visitor center, including a new bat exhibit, is open 9:00 a.m. to 5:00 p.m. CST. Park is open from 8:00 a.m. to sunset.

***Directions:*** *Park is three miles north of Marianna on Florida Highway 166.*

DeLorme Map 32

**Ownership:** Department of Environmental Protection (850) 482-9598
**Size:** 1,284 acres
**Closest town:** Marianna

*The pipistrelle is one of 16 bat species found in Florida. All are harmless to humans. Each adult bat captures at least 400 or more insects nightly; a moderate-sized summer colony of 20,000 individuals may consume eight million mosquitoes, beetles, moths, and other nocturnal pests each night. Look for tiny bat silhouettes fluttering against the evening sky, especially around water.*

BARRY MANSELL

# 7 ST. JOSEPH PENINSULA STATE PARK

**Description:** Visitors to this park will be impressed by the miles of white sand beaches set against a backdrop of tall dunes. The park is situated on St. Joseph spit, a long, narrow finger of land nearly parallel to the coast near Port St. Joe. The Gulf of Mexico forms the park's western boundary; St. Joseph Bay lies to the east. In October, birders come to watch migrating hawks soaring over the peninsula. This is the best spot in Florida to see peregrine falcons. The northern part of the park is designated as a wilderness preserve; only hiking and primitive camping are permitted. The park is popular with fishermen, swimmers, and campers. Large numbers of butterflies, including monarchs, pass through the park in the fall.

**Viewing Information:** After entering the park, stop at Eagle Harbor. At low tide, great blue, little blue, and tricolored herons join great and snowy egrets in these shallow waters. In the winter, this sheltered harbor may have shorebirds, red-breasted mergansers, common loons, and horned grebes. Bottled-nosed dolphins are occasionally seen offshore. Watch for migrating hawks from this part of the park or from the beach. Look for migratory warblers in the oak hammocks. Bald eagles, northern gannets, and a variety of gulls and terns are regularly seen. Skunks and raccoons make regular evening forays into the campgrounds. Look for the tracks of foxes, bobcats, and beach mice near the dunes and upper beaches. Visitors may hike into the primitive area by following the beach or a central sand road in the island's interior. Be prepared for insects, sunburn, and thirst. Rental cabins available.

**Directions:** *From Port St. Joe on U.S. Highway 98, travel 1.5 miles south to County Road 30A. Proceed south about eight miles. Turn west onto County 30-E and drive about ten miles to park entrance.*

DeLorme Map 59

**Ownership:** Department of Environmental Protection (850) 227-1327
**Size:** 2,516 acres
**Closest town:** Port St. Joe

*Raccoons are most active at night. As they search shallow saltwater and freshwater habitats for small fish, crabs, frogs, insects, and berries, they leave five-toed footprints in the soft sand and mud. Check in the early morning for evidence of their meanderings.*

ART WOLFE

**Description:** This large, completely undeveloped barrier island, located just west of the mouth of the Apalachicola River in Franklin County, offers eighty miles of sand roads for hiking and wildlife viewing. St. Vincent is accessible only by boat, and preserves seventeen different habitat types and a great variety of native wildlife. In addition, an introduced population of sambar deer, an elk native to Southeast Asia, roams the island, coexisting with the much smaller native white-tailed deer. Shy, free-ranging, endangered red wolves are being bred here as well.

**Viewing Information:** In the winter months, waterfowl populations peak on interior freshwater lakes and ponds. Nesting bald eagles may be spotted in pines near marshes and lakes. March through May, watch for nesting ospreys and wood ducks. Migrating songbirds use this and other Gulf Coast islands to rest and feed before and after their trans-Gulf flights. In summer, walk the beach to observe "crawls" from night nesting sea turtles, as well as a great variety of shorebirds, including oystercatchers and black skimmers. Peregrine falcons are among the numerous species of raptors that may be seen during fall migration, September through November.

**Directions:** *Travel eight miles west from Apalachicola on U.S. Highway 98 to County Road 30A. Turn left and drive about ten miles to County Road 30B. The boat ramp is at the end of the road. Contact Apalachicola Chamber of Commerce (850-653-9419) to arrange boat transportation to St. Vincent for a nominal fee. The refuge is open during daylight hours only.*

DeLorme Maps 59 and 60

**Ownership:** U.S. Fish and Wildlife Service (850) 653-8808
**Size:** 12,358 acres
**Closest town:** Apalachicola

*The endangered red wolf was once found throughout the southeastern U.S. By 1980, the species was extinct in the wild due to expanding human populations and extensive land clearing. Today the red wolf exists only in experimental populations in a handful of national wildlife refuges and small island propagation projects.*

JEFF FOOTT

# 9 ST. GEORGE ISLAND STATE PARK

**Description:** Surrounded by Apalachicola Bay and the Gulf of Mexico, this narrow island park offers nine miles of unspoiled beaches and dry forests to recreationists and wildlife watchers.

**Viewing Information:** American oystercatchers, willets, spotted sandpipers, ruddy turnstones, sanderlings, dunlins, and four plover species, including nesting snowy plovers, are often spotted on the beach. Ring-billed and laughing gulls, and Forster's and royal terns are present year-round. Bald eagles and ospreys nest in the park. Look for loons, scoters, mergansers, and northern gannets off the beach in winter. Other wintering waterfowl includes redheads, lesser scaup, and bufflehead. At low tide, look at the water's edge on the bay side of the island for great and snowy egrets, and great blue, tricolored, and little blue herons year-round. During spring and fall, St. George is famous among birders for its migrant songbirds, hawks, and falcons. Thirty-three wood warbler and seven vireo species are regularly seen; look in the trees near the youth campground. Sharp-shinned hawks, northern harriers, American kestrels, and peregrine falcons pause here during migration, especially after cold fronts. Many loggerhead turtles nest on the beach during summer.

*Directions: From U.S. Highway 98 at Eastpoint, travel south across the bridge and causeway. On the island, turn left; follow road about 4.5 miles to park entrance.*

DeLorme Maps 60 and 61

**Ownership:** Department of Environmental Protection (850) 927-2111
**Size:** 1,962 acres
**Closest town:** Eastpoint

*Elongated bills and aerodynamic bodies enable black skimmers to capture small fish while in flight. Undisturbed barrier islands, a disappearing resource in Florida, are traditional nesting grounds for black skimmers.* MICHAEL S. SAMPLE

**Description:** *AUTO TOUR.* This 31-mile loop in the southwest portion of the forest follows the paved roads of the Apalachee Savannahs Scenic Byway. The longleaf pine flatwoods, cypress swamps, and prairie savannahs offer rare and unusual plant communities with spectacular seasonal wildflower displays. There are more federally-listed endangered red-cockaded woodpecker colonies in this forest than anyplace else in the world.

**Viewing Information:** The red-cockaded woodpecker is found throughout the forest in mature stands of longleaf pine with an open understory. The forest is also a good place to see pileated, red-bellied, and downy woodpeckers, as well as pine warblers, brown-headed nuthatches, Bachman's sparrows, and northern bobwhites. Late spring and early fall are the best times to observe birds and wildflowers. Pitcher plant bogs reach their peak bloom in April and May. *AVOID TRAMPLING THESE FRAGILE PLANT COMMUNITIES.* It is not uncommon to see fox squirrels, wild turkey, and white-tailed deer on evening or early morning drives. Purchase a detailed forest map at the Wakulla Ranger District office on Florida Highway 319, north of Crawfordville, or at the Apalachicola Ranger District office in Bristol on Florida 20. Both offices open Monday through Friday 8:00 a.m. to 4:00 p.m. Seasonal hunting may affect access. Entrance fees assessed in some recreation areas and campgrounds.

*Directions: From Bristol, go south about 12 miles on County Road 12 to intersection with County 379. Driving loop begins here. See map.*

DeLorme Maps 48 and 49

**Ownership:** USDA Forest Service: (850) 926-3561 or (850) 643-2283
**Size:** 563,668 acres
**Closest town:** Bristol

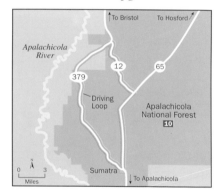

The endangered red-cockaded woodpecker travels in family groups and excavates cavities in living pines, principally longleaf pine infected with red-heart disease. Florida's three national forests support substantial populations of this bird.

BILL LEA

## 11 WAKULLA SPRINGS STATE PARK AND LODGE

**Description:** Wakulla Springs is one of the world's largest and deepest freshwater springs. From deep within North Florida's limestone interior, cold, clean water gushes forth to form the Wakulla River. The river runs through old-growth cypress swamp with abundant bird and reptile life in the water and along the shore. Nature trails in the upland portion of the park traverse floodplain and hardwood forests. Ranger-led boat tours provide views of the river; glass-bottom boats allow vistors to see large schools of fish in the spring. A popular swimming and snorkeling area.

**Viewing Information:** This site offers excellent wildlife viewing at close range. On the River cruise, look for anhingas, double-crested cormorants, common moorhens, purple gallinules, great blue, little blue, and green-backed herons, great and snowy egrets, white ibis, and limpkins. In winter, wood ducks, American wigeons, greater and lesser scaup, and American coot are common. Snakes, turtles, and American alligators of all sizes are regularly seen basking on the riverbank and other exposed vegetation. White-tailed deer and wild turkey are seen occasionally on shore. Bald eagles, red-shoulderd hawks, ospreys, and black and turkey vultures soar overhead. Watch for Mississippi and swallow-tailed kites in spring and summer.

**Directions:** *From Tallahassee, take U.S. Highway 319 or Florida Highway 61 south. Two miles beyond Capital Circle, take left fork onto Florida 61 and travel 7.5 miles to Florida 267. Take left, then immediate right into park entrance.*

DeLorme Map 50

**Ownership:** Department of Environmental Protection (850) 224-5950
**Size:** 2,860 acres
**Closest town:** Tallahassee

*Quiet exploration of a freshwater marsh can reward wildlife viewers with this magnificent sight: the stunning, iridescent plumage of a purple gallinule. Extremely long toes enable the secretive gallinule to walk delicately on floating plants.*

LARRY LIPSKY

**Description:** Birding opportunities abound in the extensive salt and brackish marshes, hardwood swamps, pine flatwoods, and pine/oak uplands bordering Apalachee Bay. Diked impoundments attract many species of wintering waterfowl. Numerous trails for hiking and bicycling.

**Viewing Information:** Drive Lighthouse Road from the visitor center to historic St. Marks Lighthouse. The road provides easy access to dike trails and the Mounds Interpretive Nature Trail. Look for wading birds and waterfowl in pools alongside the road. Try some of the hikes down the dikes to Stoney Bayou and Mounds Pools. Look for bald eagles, ospreys, and belted kingfishers on snags and exposed perches. Shorebirds, brown pelicans, ring-billed and laughing gulls, and Forster's terns prefer the beach and pilings near the lighthouse. American alligators are common. Bobcat, river otter, and white-tailed deer are best viewed at sunrise and sunset. Several species of butterflies migrate through the refuge in September and October; heaviest concentrations on flowers and shrubs near lighthouse. Interpretive guide available for seven-mile wildlife drive. Seasonal hunting may affect access to portions of refuge. *EXCELLENT VISITOR CENTER,* open Monday through Friday 8:00 a.m. to 4:00 p.m., weekends 10 a.m. to 5 p.m. Closed on federal holidays.

*Directions: From Tallahassee, take Florida Highway 363 south to Wakulla. Turn left onto Florida 267 and drive 3.5 miles to U.S. Highway 98. Turn left and drive 0.5 mile; turn south on Lighthouse Road to refuge entrance.*

DeLorme Maps 50 and 51

**Ownership:** U.S. Fish and Wildlife Service (850) 925-6121
**Size:** 68,000 acres
**Closest town:** St. Marks

*To identify the male blue-winged teal, look for a crescent-shaped white patch behind the bill. Females are mottled brown. In flight, look for flashing, powder-blue wing patches on both sexes. Florida's most abundant and widely-distributed winter duck, teal arrive as early as late July and remain until April or May.* HELEN LONGEST-SLAUGHTER

# 13 BIG BEND WILDLIFE MANAGEMENT AREA: HICKORY MOUND IMPOUNDMENT

**Description:** Hickory Mound features a large, brackish impoundment on the coast of the Gulf of Mexico encircled by a 6.5-mile dike. Prescribed burning and manipulation of water levels produce excellent wintering habitat inside the levee, attracting concentrations of waterfowl and wading birds. Bald eagles and ospreys nest in palm and pine hammocks that dot the landscape.

**Viewing Information:** Drive or walk the levee to view a diversity of waterfowl, including green- and blue-winged teal, northern pintail, gadwall, mallard, American wigeon, northern shoveler, black duck, canvasback, redhead, ring-necked duck, lesser and greater scaup, common goldeneye, bufflehead, and hooded and red-breasted merganser. Snow geese and swans overwinter occasionally; American coots and common moorhens can be plentiful. White pelicans occur sporadically year-round. During spring and summer months, swallow-tailed and Mississippi kites, orchard orioles, and gray kingbirds are commonly spotted. From the observation tower, bald eagle and ospreys and their nests are easy to observe. Monarch butterflies gather here during their fall migration. Wading birds, including white ibis, double-crested cormorants, wood storks, great and little blue herons, great and snowy egrets, and tricolored herons, yellow-crowned night herons, and green-backed herons nest nearby and are highly visible. American alligators visible on warm days year-round. *MANAGED HUNTS UNTIL NOON ON MONDAY, WEDNESDAY, AND FRIDAY, SEPTEMBER THROUGH JANUARY. CALL AHEAD FOR HUNT DATES AND REGULATIONS SUMMARY. LIMEROCK ROADS ROUGH BUT PASSABLE.*

***Directions:*** *Eighteen miles west of Perry on U.S. Highway 98, turn left on Cow Creek Grade. Travel six miles on limerock road to check station for map and regulations summary. Proceed two miles to impoundment.*

DeLorme Map 51

**Ownership:** Florida Game and Fresh Water Fish Commission (850) 838-1306 or (850) 758-0525
**Size:** 1,834 acres
**Closest town:** Econfina

Because of the loss of wetland habitats in Florida, artificial impoundments have been created to provide critical feeding, nesting, and resting areas for wading birds, waterfowl, and shorebirds. Wildlife viewing can be excellent in these areas, particularly in winter, when waterfowl concentrations reach their peak. Visit Hickory Mound Impoundment (see above), the Guana River Wildlife Management Area, and St. Marks and Loxahatchee national wildlife refuges for excellent bird watching, and evaluate the effectiveness of this management tool.

## 14 BIG BEND WILDLIFE MANAGEMENT AREA: HAGEN'S COVE

**Description:** Enjoy panoramic views of the pine islands and shallow bays of the Gulf of Mexico at this locally well-known recreation area. The unique natural beaches of Hagen's Cove are extremely rare along the Big Bend coast. Exposed mudflats in bays to the north and south of the parking area host huge numbers of shore and wading birds at low tide.

**Viewing Information:** A great variety of shore and wading birds may be viewed year-round, with increases during migration and strong west winds. Plovers, sandpipers, marbled godwit, willet, American oystercatcher, dunlin, short-billed dowitcher, and whimbrel gather here during spring and fall migration. Reddish egrets are sometimes spotted during late summer and fall. Special summer sightings include magnificent frigatebirds, American swallow-tailed kites, and gray kingbirds. Bald eagles nest nearby and often soar overhead. Osprey and brown pelicans fish year-round. Wintering waterfowl include bufflehead, red-breasted merganser, redhead, lesser scaup, and common goldeneye. The observation tower south of the parking area offers a good view of area bays. Bring a spotting scope. Boat ramp provides high-tide access to Gulf of Mexico.

**Directions:** *Travel about 4.5 miles south of Perry on Florida Highway 27A. Turn right on County Road 361 and drive twenty-two miles to Hagen's Cove Road. Turn right and proceed 1.5 miles to parking area.*

DeLorme Map 62

**Ownership:** Florida Game and Fresh Water Fish Commission (850) 838-1306 or (850) 758-0525
**Size:** 5 acres
**Closest town:** Keaton Beach

*The dunlin uses its long, thick bill to pick and probe for marine worms, crustaceans, and mollusks along Florida's beaches and tidal flats. Dunlins are common on the Gulf and Atlantic coasts from late summer through early spring.*
JOHN GERLACH

## 15 ANDREWS WILDLIFE MANAGEMENT AREA

**Description:** This tract contains one of Florida's largest remaining hardwood hammock forests. Three Florida Champion trees have been recorded in this old-growth forest: persimmon, Florida maple, and river birch. Eight hundred acres of river bottomland bordering the Suwannee River add diversity. Many wildlife species are abundant, including white-tailed deer, wild turkey, bobcat, coyote, and gray and southern flying squirrels. Eventual conversion of nearby slash pine plantations to longleaf pine will further improve wildlife habitat.

**Viewing Information:** Several narrow but passable dirt roads and trails traverse the area, along with six walking nature trails; obtain maps at interpretive kiosk near entrance. Five clearings and scattered roadside openings have been planted in grasses and grain to attract wildlife. Check these areas early or late in the day for white-tailed deer and wild turkey. Red-shouldered hawks, barred and screech owls are common year-round. Watch overhead for American swallow-tailed and Mississippi kites during spring and summer. Excellent migratory songbird viewing during April and October along the river, roads, and trails. Look for gopher tortoise burrows in the open food plot areas. Note diggings of a large population of wild pigs.

*Directions: From Chiefland, travel north 4.7 miles on U.S. Highway 19. Turn left onto County Road 211 and drive 0.9 mile to entrance kiosk.*

DeLorme map 64

**Ownership:** Florida Game and Fresh Water Fish Commission (352) 493-6020 or (352) 758-0525
**Size:** 3,501 acres
**Closest town:** Chiefland

*Male white-tailed deer begin growing new antlers each spring. During the summer, antlers grow inside a "velvet" covering which dries up in the fall and is rubbed off against trees. At first the new antlers look bare and bloody, but continued rubbing eventually polishes them white.* GAIL SHUMWAY

## 16 LOWER SUWANNEE NATIONAL WILDLIFE REFUGE

**Description:** This refuge, adjacent to the Cedar Keys National Wildlife Refuge, flanks the lower 20 miles of the Suwannee River and fronts 26 miles of the Gulf of Mexico, making it one of the largest undeveloped river delta–estuarine systems in the United States.

**Viewing Information:** Extensive walking and biking trails, miles of limerock roads, and ample boating opportunities provide access to the variety of habitats at this refuge. Near the refuge office, walk the 0.6-mile River Trail through hardwood swamp to a boardwalk and river overlook. Morning or evening drives along interior roads may afford glimpses of turkey and deer in the uplands. Scan interior sloughs for wintering waterfowl. Ospreys, swallow-tailed kites, and bald eagles nest in the refuge and are regularly observed. The 1.0-mile Dennis Creek Loop Trail passes through oak and pine sand ridges skirting the edge of the salt marsh. Listen for rails and watch for wading birds. A boardwalk at the end of the Shell Mound area allows viewing of numerous birds including black skimmers, American oystercatchers, willets, sanderlings, gulls, and terns. The Salt Creek Boardwalk and Overlook provides a breathtaking view of the salt marsh and coastal pine islands. The refuge office is open 7:30 a.m. to 4:00 p.m. weekdays. Call ahead for maps, seasonal hunt dates, and regulations. For boat rentals or guided nature tours of this area, contact the Cedar Key (352-543-5600) or the Suwannee (352-542-7349) chambers of commerce.

***Directions:*** *See map*

DeLorme Map 69

**Ownership:** U.S. Fish and Wildlife Service (352) 493-0238
**Size:** 52,257 acres
**Closest town:** Chiefland

*Historically, swallow-tailed kites nested in forested wetlands in 21 states, from Florida north along the corridor of the Mississippi to Minnesota. The bird's range contracted sharply around the turn of the century due to wanton shooting and the draining and logging of its habitat, the nation's great river swamps. Florida remains this elegant raptor's breeding stronghold.*

JEFF RIPPLE

## 17 THE CEDAR KEYS

**Description:** The Cedar Keys are a group of islands set in the Gulf of Mexico, about 15 miles south of the mouth of the Suwannee River. The approach to the picturesque fishing village of Cedar Key passes through thousands of acres of pine flatwoods, sand pine scrub, and salt marsh. The shoreline along the coast here is a maze of tidal creeks within large expanses of salt marsh. Several of the dozen offshore keys serve as refuge and breeding grounds for thousands of wading birds, one of the largest nesting areas in Florida. To protect the nesting birds, access to Seahorse Key is prohibited from March 1– June 31.

**Viewing Information:** Exploration of the area by car begins east of town on Florida Highway 24. Turn north onto Florida 347 and go about three miles to Florida 326. Turn left and, after a mile or so, begin to check the scrub vegetation and power lines alongside the road for the curious scrub jay. Gopher tortoise burrows are commonly seen. Return to Florida 24 and drive towards the town of Cedar Key. Pull over near the first bridge and scan the mudflats at low tide for numerous wading birds: white ibis, great and snowy egrets, great blue, little blue, tricolored herons, and wintering waterfowl are common here. Double-crested cormorants, bald eagles, ospreys, and brown pelicans may be seen over the marshes and tidal creeks. Private boaters should call the Cedar Keys National Wildlife Refuge office in Chiefland (904-493-0238) for access regulations. The Cedar Key Chamber of Commerce office (904-543-5600) has information on boating and canoeing trips. *ISLAND INTERIORS OFF-LIMITS.*

**Directions:** *From Chiefland, go south on U.S. Highway 98 to Otter Creek. Turn right onto Florida 24 and follow signs to the town of Cedar Key.*

DeLorme map 69

**Ownership:** U.S. Fish and Wildlife Service (352) 493-0238
**Closest town:** Cedar Key

*On the Gulf Coast, salt marshes are the primary natural community from Apalachicola Bay south to Tampa Bay. Within the marsh vegetation, many young fish, shellfish, and crustaceans find refuge and food.* FRED WHITEHEAD

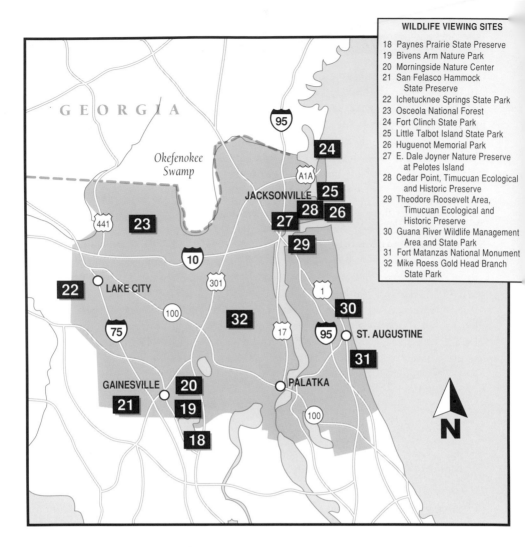

WILDLIFE VIEWING SITES

18 Paynes Prairie State Preserve
19 Bivens Arm Nature Park
20 Morningside Nature Center
21 San Felasco Hammock
   State Preserve
22 Ichetucknee Springs State Park
23 Osceola National Forest
24 Fort Clinch State Park
25 Little Talbot Island State Park
26 Huguenot Memorial Park
27 E. Dale Joyner Nature Preserve
   at Pelotes Island
28 Cedar Point, Timucuan Ecological
   and Historic Preserve
29 Theodore Roosevelt Area,
   Timucuan Ecological and
   Historic Preserve
30 Guana River Wildlife Management
   Area and State Park
31 Fort Matanzas National Monument
32 Mike Roess Gold Head Branch
   State Park

## REGION TWO: NORTHEAST

The Osceola National Forest anchors a sprawling wilderness which extends north through Pinhook Swamp to the great Okefenokee Swamp in Georgia. This region supports rare, wide-ranging species such as black bear, bobcat, and the swallow-tailed kite.

Along the Atlantic coast lies a protective fringe of sea islands, sandy dunes, and beaches. Large concentrations of nesting terns, black skimmers, and shorebirds compete with the growing human population for beachfront nesting and wintering sites. Manatees gather in the warm waters west of Amelia Island and Fernandina Beach, and in the Amelia River.

Along the north-flowing St. Johns River, abundant wildlife populations thrive, including river otters, bald eagles, wood storks, and other wading birds. The Paynes Prairie basin annually attracts up to 2,000 overwintering sandhill cranes. Upland scrub and sandhill communities in Putnam and Clay counties provide habitat for kestrels, gopher tortoises, red-cockaded woodpeckers, and a diversity of rare flowering plants.

**Description:** Visitors traveling south on Interstate 75 or U.S. Highway 441 from Gainesville can't miss the dramatic vista that greets them when the road descends onto the broad, flat Paynes Prairie basin. This preserve is covered by marsh and wet prairie vegetation with acres of open water. Year-round resident Florida sandhill cranes are joined by thousands of migratory greater sandhill cranes in the winter. The highlight of a winter visit to this site, particularly at dawn or dusk, is to hear the bugling calls of these magnificent long-legged birds. Uplands along the rim of the prairie include pine flatwoods, oak hammocks, and ponds. Alligators, snakes, and wading birds are common. Bison have been reintroduced and may occasionally be seen.

**Viewing Information:** From the southern edge of the prairie on U.S. Highway 441, park and hike the Bolen Bluff Trail. This loop trail passes through hardwood hammock where the calls of great horned owls and red-bellied woodpeckers, plus a variety of woodland species, may be heard year-round. White-tailed deer are occasionally seen. Before the trail loops back, there is access down onto the prairie via a grassy berm. Snakes are common. Red-winged blackbirds noisily proclaim their presence from shrubbery alongside the trail. Continue south on U.S. 441 to the entrance to the Lake Wauberg Recreation Area and the visitor center and observation tower. The tower overlooks the prairie and provides good views of northern harriers and sandhill cranes in the winter. Look for red-shouldered and red-tailed hawks, bald eagles, and black and turkey vultures year-round. There is a short nature trail near the visitor center. Lake Wauberg is popular for canoeing and fishing. Numerous hiking, biking, and horse trails. Inquire about seasonal ranger-led walks and overnight backpacking trips. Call (352) 466-4100 for more information.

*Directions: Go south on U.S. 441 from Gainesville across Paynes Prairie basin. Parking for Bolen Bluff Trail is 3.5 miles south of Florida Highway 331 on the east side of U.S. 441. The Lake Wauberg Recreation Area is four miles farther south.*

DeLorme Map 65

**Ownership:** Department of Environmental Protection (352) 466-3397
**Size:** 21,000 acres
**Closest town:** Gainesville/Micanopy

Florida's climate supports 127 native species of reptiles and amphibians, one of the richest concentrations of any state in the country. There are only six species of venomous snakes in Florida (two are very rare and found only in extreme north Florida) and the incidence of snake bite is low. Nonetheless, visitors should use common sense and stay alert: almost every natural habitat in Florida supports at least one species of poisonous snake. Give all snakes a wide berth and leave snake handling up to the experts.

**Description:** Freshwater marsh and mature live oak hammock provide a quiet preserve on the edge of nearby Paynes Prairie. An excellent interpretive kiosk explains both altered and natural aspects of this small urban park.

**Viewing Information:** A 1,200-foot boardwalk encircles a marsh that draws common moorhens, purple gallinules, common yellowthroats, aquatic turtles, and banded water snakes. Wading birds, including great blue and little blue herons, and great, cattle, and snowy egrets use the marsh year-round. American alligators nest in the marsh; hatchlings may be visible close to interpretive kiosks in late summer. On the hammock trail and around the picnic area, barred and great horned owls are commonly heard and seen; eastern screech owls occur less frequently. Hermit thrushes, American redstarts, and other migratory songbirds pass through the preserve in April and October. Bobcats, seen infrequently, thrive on the park's population of gray squirrels. Listen for calling sandhill cranes on the nearby prairie and larger marshes in winter and early spring. Open seven days a week, 9:00 a.m. to 5:00 p.m.

**Directions:** *Take exit 74 from Interstate 75 south of Gainesville. Turn east onto Florida Highway 331 (Williston Road) and drive 2.5 miles to Main Street. Go north 0.25 mile on Main; park entrance is on the left (west) side of road.*

DeLorme Map 65

**Ownership:** City of Gainesville (352) 334-2231
**Size:** 54 acres
**Closest town:** Gainesville

*Barred owls live in woodlands and forested swamps throughout the state. Old hawk or squirrel nests, along with tree cavities, are preferred nest sites. Listen for this owl's distinctive call of "Who cooks for you? Who cooks for you all?", especially as nesting begins in the early winter months.*
BILL LEA

**Description:** This 278-acre longleaf pine/turkey oak preserve includes seven miles of nature trails and a boardwalk through a cypress dome. Wildflowers are abundant seasonally and a number of endangered plants and animals live within the park.

**Viewing Information:** Morningside's upland sandhills and pine flatwoods are fire-dependent communities that must burn regularly to function well. Gopher tortoise, fox squirrel, rose orchid, and longleaf pine are adapted to frequent burning cycles and thrive here. Mound-forming southeastern pocket gophers, eastern diamondback rattlesnakes, and rufous-sided towhees may also be found on the sandhill trails. The Bachman's sparrow, pine warbler, eastern bluebird, brown-headed nuthatch, red-headed woodpecker, northern bob-white, and American kestrel are typical flatwoods species observed in this sanctuary. During spring and summer, look in the cypress dome for great crested flycatchers, prothonotary warblers, and pileated woodpeckers. Fall wildflowers stimulated by regular summer burning attract dozens of butterfly species. Nature center, turn-of-the-century farm, many guided classes and activities. Open seven days a week, 9:00 a.m. to 5:00 p.m.

**Directions:** *From U.S. Highway 441 in Gainesville, travel east 3.5 miles on East University Avenue. Sanctuary is on north side of road.*

DeLorme 65

**Ownership:** City of Gainesville (352) 334-2170
**Size:** 278 acres
**Closest town:** Gainesville

*Fall is the season for butterfly watchers in Florida. Look for the leisurely flight of giant swallowtails (above), and dozens of other species as they seek nectar from asters, goldenrod, blazing star, and other native wildflowers. Unmowed roadside ditches, pinewoods, and open fields are good places to look for butterflies, especially from August through November.* JACK MESSLER

**Description:** Nearly every major north Florida forest type occurs on this un-developed but outstanding natural area. One of the finest woodlands in north Florida, with its limestone outcrops, sinkholes, and hilly elevation, shelters southern magnolia, American holly, spruce pine, and Florida maple. Unique to San Felasco is Sanchez Prairie, a large basin forested with a swamp of unusual planar and pop ash trees. Numerous ponds, streams, marshes, and sinkholes scattered throughout. Champion trees and many rare plants thrive here. The diverse plant communities provide favorable conditions for bobcat, gray fox, white-tailed deer, many songbirds, and wild turkey.

**Viewing Information:** Wood thrush, hooded, and prothonotary warblers nest May through August. Excellent birding during fall and spring migrations. American redstart, blackpoll, ovenbird, yellow-bellied sapsucker, and black-throated blue warblers pass through the preserve April-May, and again September-October. Migratory waterfowl, including teal, mergansers, wood ducks, and mallards, dabble and dive in ponds November-April. Many wading birds nest here, including great and little blue herons, white ibis, and wood storks. Quiet, patient observers may spot hawks, owls, wild turkey, and white-tailed deer year-round. Look for gopher tortoises in sandhill areas. Miles of marked and unmarked foot trails.

**Directions:** *Preserve is located four miles northwest of Gainesville on County Road 232 (Millhopper Road).*

DeLorme Map 65

**Ownership:** Department of Environmental Protection (904) 462-7905
**Size:** 6,900 acres
**Closest town:** Gainesville

*This most beautiful of song-birds, the hooded warbler, is heard far more often than seen. Listen for its ringing song of "weeta, weeta, weet-ee-o" during the spring months, in migration, or on nesting territories in dense swamplands of northern Florida.*

WILLIAM J. WEBER

**Description:** Nine crystal-clear springs feed this small, much-beloved river. The river flows southwest for six miles before it joins the Santa Fe River, passing alternately through green bowers of hammock and river swamp. Many kinds of fish, turtles, and wading birds may be spotted along the river's winding course. Near upland trails, wild turkey, songbirds, white-tailed deer, gopher tortoise, and fox squirrels reside in the sandhills.

**Viewing Information:** A quiet float in a rented tube or canoe may yield sightings of limpkin, wood duck, river otter, or beaver. Look aloft for swallow-tailed kites in spring and summer. Park personnel recommend visitors canoe from the headsprings canoe launch to the last take-out above the U.S. Highway 27 bridge, about 3.5 miles. Tubers are urged to use the park's south entrance and float the lower stretch to lessen the impact on the narrow, shallow reaches of the upper river. A free in-park tram operates from the south end parking area May through September. Bring a mask and snorkel to view fish and turtles. Guided moonlight canoe trips offered seasonally; reservations required. Two self-guided trails at the north entrance of the park offer views of the river, and wind through pine and oak-dominated sandhill communities. Equipment rentals are available outside the park. *AVOID VISITING JUNE THROUGH AUGUST; RIVER RECEIVES HEAVY USE.*

**Directions:** *See map*

DeLorme Map 64

**Ownership:** Department of Environmental Protection (904) 497-2511
**Size:** 2,241 acres
**Closest town:** Fort White

*The Florida red-bellied turtle is commonly spotted basking on logs or snags in many rivers and ponds. Watch these large turtles from a distance, since they are quick to slide off their sunning perches and disappear.*

HELEN LONGEST-SLAUGHTER

**Description:** *AUTO TOUR.* This drive through the forest passes several colony sites of the federally-listed endangered red-cockaded woodpecker. Two short walks off of this route are also described. Longleaf and slash pine woods, and cypress and bay swamps characterize this large, intensively-managed forest.

**Viewing Information and Directions:** Purchase a detailed forest map at the ranger station, open Monday through Friday 8:00 a.m. to 4:00 p.m.; station located on U.S. Highway 90, just west of Olustee (see map below). To start the driving tour, travel west on U.S. 90, 3.8 miles from the ranger station to the Mount Carrie Wayside Park and the start of a one-mile-long walking trail into the pinewoods. Red-cockaded woodpecker trees are marked with a broad, white band and trees actively used by the birds are identified by their profuse sap flow. *RESPECT THE ENDANGERED STATUS OF THIS BIRD—DO NOT APPROACH CAVITY TREES.* Pinewoods throughout this forest abound with rufous-sided towhees, Bachman's sparrows, pine warblers, brown-headed nuthatches, northern bobwhite, rattlesnakes, and fox squirrels. From the wayside park, continue west on U.S. 90 and drive the large circular route illustrated on the map. There are several red-cockaded woodpecker colony sites along here. Return to U.S. 90 and go east to Forest Road 250A, a paved road. Follow signs to the Ocean Pond campground. Just before the campground, the Florida Trail crosses the road. Look for orange blazes on the trees. Walk north along the trail for several hundred yards to a cypress swamp boardwalk. Listen for pileated woodpeckers and a variety of warblers. Look for wild turkey, white-tailed deer, gray fox, and bobcat on dawn or dusk drives. American swallow-tailed kites may be seen soaring over open areas in spring and summer. Restrooms are located at the Olustee Recreation Area. During hunting season (November to January), visitors are required to stay on numbered roads south of Interstate 10. Wear a bright orange vest if hiking in the forest during these months.

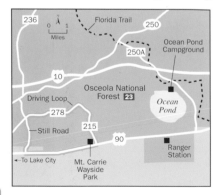

DeLorme Map 55

**Ownership:** USDA Forest Service (904) 752-2577
**Size:** 190,000 acres
**Closest town:** Lake City

The Osceola is the smallest of Florida's three national forests. About one-half of its 190,000 acres are classified as forested swamp or wetland. To the north, Pinhook Swamp and Georgia's Okefenokee Swamp National Wildlife Refuge join the Osceola to provide an important wildlife corridor.

**NORTHEAST**

**Description:** Fort Clinch is situated at the northern tip of Amelia Island, Florida's northernmost Atlantic barrier island. The park is bordered by the Amelia River to the west, and the Atlantic Ocean to the east. The St. Mary's River channel on the north narrowly separates the park from Cumberland Island, Ga. Amelia Island typifies the coastal habitats that define so much of the southeastern United States. Salt marshes and meandering tidal creeks, high dunes, Atlantic beaches, and coastal hammocks characterize these rich and productive marine habitats. Canoeing is a wonderful way to explore the quiet tidal creeks. Look for hermit crabs, wading birds, and rails. Visits to historic Fort Clinch, camping, swimming, fishing, and hiking through coastal hammock and along the beach are the main visitor activities.

**Viewing Information:** Take a walk on the long pier that juts out into Cumberland Sound from the park's northeast corner. It parallels a stone jetty, a popular loafing spot for double-crested cormorants and brown pelicans. Scan the shoreline on both sides of the pier for laughing, ring-billed, herring and great black-backed gulls, royal terns, and shorebirds. Two loops of the Willow Pond Nature Trail wind through a coastal hammock and encircle a small pond where turtles and alligators may be found. Check here for spring migrant and typical woodland birds. Look for painted buntings in the summer.

**Directions:** *The entrance to the park is approximately 1.5 miles north of Fernandina Beach on Florida Highway A1A.*

DeLorme Map 41

**Ownership:** Department of Environmental Protection (904) 277-7274
**Size:** 1,153 acres
**Closest town:** Fernandina Beach

*Brown pelicans are familiar sights around coastal Florida, and some have grown accustomed to begging or pirating bait and catch waste. Entanglement with fish hooks and monofilament line kill or maim hundreds of pelicans each year. If a bird becomes hooked, reel it in, hold the bird by the bill, fold the wings against the body and carefully remove the hook.*

BARBARA GERLACH

**Description:** This Atlantic barrier island on the coast between Fernandina Beach and Jacksonville has a magnificent beach and dune complex. Behind it lies a thick coastal hardwood hammock whose live oak and cedar trees may be several centuries old. On the sheltered bayside, extensive salt marshes are dissected by tidal creeks—habitat for raccoons and river otters, as well as great and snowy egrets, and great blue herons. Clapper rails prey on the great herds of fiddler crabs among the stalks of saltmarsh cordgrass.

**Viewing Information:** A 1.5-mile trail leaves from the south side of the campground and explores the salt marshes on the island's western side. Expect to see herons and egrets hunting small fish and crabs. A four-mile trail leaves from near the park's entrance station and traverses hammock and beach. Look for snakes, gopher tortoises, painted buntings, and migratory warblers and shorebirds. Loggerhead turtles nest along these beaches in the summer. From the observation deck/pier at the south end of the island, watch for brown pelicans, laughing and ring-billed gulls, royal terns, and sea ducks, such as bufflehead, common goldeneye, and scoters. *PREPARE FOR THIRST AND INSECTS.*

**Directions:** *From Interstate 95 in Jacksonville, go east on Heckscher Drive (County Road 105) until it becomes Florida Highway A1A and turns north along the coast; follow signs to park. From the Jacksonville beaches to the south, take the ferry at Mayport across the St. Johns River to County 105/Florida A1A and go east. For ferry schedules, call (904) 246-2922.*

DeLorme Map 58

**Ownership:** Department of Environmental Protection (904) 251-2320
**Size:** 2,500 acres
**Closest town:** Jacksonville

*Tidal creeks meander through extensive salt marshes on the landward side of Little Talbot Island. Many animals, including oysters, fish, and birds, spend all or part of their lives in these areas, known as estuaries.* FRED WHITEHEAD

**NORTHEAST**

**Description:** Visitors to this park are an interesting mixture of avid birders and local recreationists. Both groups are attracted to the Atlantic beaches and dunes, the jetty near the mouth of the St. Johns River, and the long sand spit that juts out into the Fort George inlet. The birders, who call the area Ward's Bank, come in the winter to view the large numbers of gulls, terns, and shorebirds which congregate at the north end of the sand spit. It is permissible to drive along the inlet and the beach, but visitors be warned: there is a great risk of getting stuck in soft sand and mud, and traffic along the shoreline jeopardizes the nesting efforts of many birds. Parts of the northern end of the area are posted and closed seasonally to protect ground-nesting terns from disturbance. Wildlife officials recommend that visitors come early in the day, park in designated paved areas, and enjoy leisurely walking and birding.

**Viewing Information:** Early fall is the best season for viewing birds. The interior lagoon attracts shorebirds: dunlins, black-bellied plovers, western sandpipers, willets, ruddy turnstones, sanderlings, and American oystercatchers. The beach and mudflats at the northern tip of the sand spit may hold thousands of gulls and terns. Laughing, ring-billed, herring, and great black-backed gulls are commonly seen, as well as royal, least, and Forster's terns. Check offshore areas in the winter for northern gannets, horned grebes, red-breasted mergansers, and common loons.

**Directions:** *From downtown Jacksonville, take Interstate 95 north to Heckscher Drive. Go east for about 19 miles (1.5 miles past the Mayport Ferry slip) and turn right at the blinking yellow light.*

DeLorme map 58

**Ownership:** State of Florida and the U.S. Army Corps of Engineers; leased to City of Jacksonville (904) 251-3215
**Size:** 449 acres
**Closest town:** Jacksonville

*The royal tern is often found in large, mixed flocks of gulls and terns on Florida beaches and sandbars. This large white bird has a forked tail, a prominent bushy black crest, and large orange-yellow bill. During breeding season, adults also have a black cap and forehead.*

MICHAEL S. SAMPLE

**Description:** This preserve consists of a chain of islands that curves out into the marshlands north of the St. Johns River. Maritime hammock and the surrounding salt creeks and marshes which characterize these small sea islands attract an abundance of wildlife. Live oak, pignut hickory, cabbage palms, and red cedar visually contrast with broad expanses of salt marsh grasses. Timucuan Indian shell middens add diversity and historical significance. Several tropical plant species at the northern limits of their ranges, including coralroot orchids and wild coffee, thrive on the calcium-rich middens.

**Viewing Information:** Hike 3.2 miles of well-interpreted trails to see gray squirrels, raccoons, and resident and migratory songbirds. On Timucuan and Coffeemound Trails, look for gopher tortoises and their burrows. Many butterflies feed on wildflowers, including sulfurs, giant and black swallowtails, fritillaries, and zebras. Nesting painted buntings are a spring highlight. Clapper rails, osprey, and northern harriers are common in the salt marsh. Look for wading birds at low tide, including wood storks, snowy and great egrets, and great blue herons. Preserve open on a limited basis to groups, by reservation only. Call ahead to arrange tour and obtain map. School and other groups may choose among a range of nature walks and guided activities.

DeLorme Map 57

**Ownership:** Jacksonville Electric Authority and Florida Power and Light Company (904) 665-8856
**Size:** 350 acres
**Closest town:** Jacksonville

*Prior to human settlement, gopher tortoises were probably common throughout most of Florida. These "landlords" use strong, flattened forelimbs to excavate a tunnel about 15 feet long and six feet deep, which offers protection from fire and extreme temperatures to more than 80 other animals.* JOHN NETHERTON

## 28 | CEDAR POINT, TIMUCUAN ECOLOGICAL AND HISTORIC PRESERVE

**Description:** The Timucuan preserve includes approximately 46,000 acres of complex salt marsh ecosystem between the lower St. Johns and Nassau rivers. Cedar Point is the National Park Service's most recent addition to this preserve, which includes three other wildlife viewing sites: Theodore Roosevelt Area, Huguenot Memorial Park, and Fort Caroline National Memorial. Features at the 400-acre Cedar Point Preserve include unspoiled salt marsh vistas, maritime hammocks, and a pine plantation.

**Viewing Information:** A variety of trails accommodate visitors looking for a short stroll as well as those out for longer, more rigorous hikes. Several trails lead to scenic overlooks. Along the salt marsh trails, look for great and snowy egrets, little and great blue herons, American oystercatchers, white ibis, wood storks, and other wading birds and shorebirds. The oak hammocks are very productive areas to spot migratory warblers in the spring and fall. In summer, the pasture trail is excellent for yellow-breasted chat, blue grosbeak, indigo and painted bunting, and orchard oriole. Site enhancements such as information kiosks are planned.

**Directions:** *See map*

DeLorme Map 58

**Ownership:** National Park Service (904) 251-3537
**Size:** 400 acres
**Closest Town:** Jacksonville

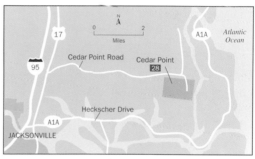

*Overgrown pastures, fields, and forest edges are favorite haunts of the indigo bunting. The brilliant blue adult male proclaims his territory throughout the summer by singing strident, high-pitched couplets from exposed perches.*
TOM VEZO

53

**Description:** Close to bustling Jacksonville, this quiet area offers four miles of hiking trails through maritime hammock and salt marsh. An observation tower at the trail midpoint offers an excellent view of scenic Round Marsh and tidal salt creeks of the St. Johns River. Timucuan Indians left thirty-five acres of shell middens on this culturally significant site. Native blueberries, subtropical wild coffee, snowberry, and green fly orchid add botanical interest.

**Viewing Information:** Brilliant painted buntings nest spring and summer in the hardwood hammock, along with barred owls, northern parula warblers, white-eyed and red-eyed vireos, and other songbirds. Osprey and red-shouldered hawks are common. Wood storks, brown pelicans, great blue herons, great and snowy egrets, and double-crested cormorants fish in the salt creek year-round. Quiet hikers may spot a raccoon or gray fox. Ranger-guided walks are available on Saturdays and Sundays. Stop first at Fort Caroline National Memorial to get a map, bird list, and other information.

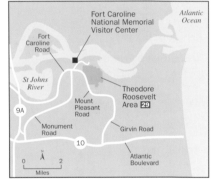

*Directions: See map*

DeLorme map 58

**Ownership:** National Park Service (904) 641-7155
**Size:** 600 acres
**Closest town:** Jacksonville

*Before Europeans colonized northwest Florida, Timucuan Indians lived in harmony with native wildlife for many centuries, though they hunted and fished extensively. Abundant wild turkeys, waterfowl, white-tailed deer, alligators, and shellfish were some of the important game animals for Timucuans and other southeastern Indians.*

FRED WHITEHEAD

# 30 GUANA RIVER WILDLIFE MANAGEMENT AREA AND STATE PARK

**Description:** This 12,000-acre, minimally-developed coastal barrier beach and sea island is bounded on the east by the Atlantic Ocean and on the west by the Tolomato River. Active wildlife management practices and an unusual diversity of plant communities account for the abundant wildlife, including 189 bird species. Guana Lake, a managed, brackish impoundment nearly ten miles long, is a popular waterfowl hunting area.

**Viewing Information:** Use a spotting scope or binoculars to observe sea ducks, northern gannets, and common loons off the ocean beach during the winter months. At the dune line and near Guana Lake, watch for migrating hawks and falcons. During April and October, especially with a west wind or after a cold front, this is the best place in northeast Florida to see peregrine falcons. Nearly 3,000-4,000 migratory ducks, American coots, common moorhens, and pied-billed grebes winter at Guana; the dam and the observation tower on Hammock Road are good spots to set up a scope. White pelicans (January and February), ospreys, and bald eagles often fish at the impounded lake. At low water levels, black-necked stilts, yellowlegs, dowitchers, and other shorebirds are abundant at the lake's north end. Try viewing from the North Beach parking lot. Big Savanna and five other managed interior ponds host wood storks, roseate spoonbills, white and glossy ibis, egrets, herons, and other water birds, especially May through September. At the Capo Creek tower, look for summering swallow-tailed kites and other raptors, as well as numerous wading birds. Raccoons and white-tailed deer feed along the marsh edge. Gopher tortoises, alligators, white-tailed deer, and a variety of snakes are commonly encountered on Guana. *BITING INSECTS AND HEAT IN SUMMER.*

**Directions:** *From St. Augustine, drive north 10.5 miles on Florida Highway A1A. Wildlife management area maps and summary of regulations are posted at all observation points. Vehicle access permitted eight days prior to seasonal hunts; remainder of the year, walk or bike only.*

DeLorme map 58

**Ownership:** Florida Game and Fresh Water Fish Commission (904) 732-1225 and Department of Environmental Protection (904) 825-5071
**Size:** 12,000 acres
**Closest town:** St. Augustine

Florida supports a tremendous diversity of wildlife species and natural communities, with a high percentage of both found nowhere else in the world. Since Florida contributes so heavily to global biological diversity, elimination of habitat and destruction of species in the state is an issue of worldwide concern.

**Description:** This small historical park is also an undiscovered natural gem. A wide variety of wildlife occupies open beach, dunes, maritime hammock, scrub, marsh, and inlet. A free ferry takes visitors to the fort on Rattlesnake Island daily, weather permitting, from 9:00 a.m. to 4:30 p.m.

**Viewing Information:** From the ferry, bottle-nosed dolphins are frequently sighted. Ospreys occur year-round, and bald eagles occasionally soar overhead during winter and spring. Cooper's hawks nest here. Belted kingfishers, brown pelicans, double-crested cormorants, and wading birds, especially great blue herons and snowy egrets, live in nearby marshes. Wood storks and roseate spoonbills are periodically seen. Gopher tortoises dig their conspicuous burrows near the 0.6-mile boardwalk nature trail. Many songbird species rest and feed in the hammock surrounding the nature trail during spring and fall migration. The parking area is a good place to look for Florida scrub-jays. In summer, look for gray kingbirds on utility wires outside park entrance on Florida Highway A1A. May through August, early risers will spot tracks of nesting loggerhead and green sea turtles on the beach. Just south of the park entrance lies an inlet with extensive tidal flats, low dunes, and wetlands. Check the sandbars for gulls, terns (Caspian, royal and least), and black skimmers at low tide. From May through July, portions of the area are closed to visitors to protect ground-nesting least terns.

**Directions:** *On Florida A1A, 15 miles south of St. Augustine.*

DeLorme Map 68

**Ownership:** National Park Service (904) 471-0116
**Size:** 298 acres
**Closest town:** Summer Haven

*The white ibis is the most recent addition to Florida's list of threatened species. Formerly the state's most abundant wading bird, the white ibis has declined precipitously in response to degradation and loss of wetlands. The bird's uniformly white plumage, red face, and down-curved bill are unmistakable.* JOHN NETHERTON

**Description:** This park is a delightful study in contrasts. A broad expanse of longleaf pine and turkey oak in the dry, rolling sandhills is bisected by a lush ravine, carved by spring-fed Gold Head Branch stream. Ferns and wildflowers carpet the steep ravine beneath a canopy of live oaks, hickories, and sweet gums. The stream empties into Lake Johnson, a popular local fishing, canoeing, and swimming spot which becomes very crowded on summer weekends. There are three other small lakes and two nature trails in the park. Canoe rentals in summer. Rental cabins available.

**Viewing Information:** To explore the ravine, hike the Ridge Trail. This is a good spot to look for foraging groups of birds called *feeding guilds*, particularly in the winter. Yellow-rumped warblers, Carolina chickadees, tufted titmice, downy woodpeckers, blue-gray gnatcatchers, and other songbirds may be found moving together through the forest—their combined vocalizations make them easy to locate. This is also a good place to find thrushes: the hermit thrush in winter, the wood thrush in summer. The flute-like song of the latter is a delight to hear. The upper slope of the ravine may have rufous-sided towhees and summer tanagers. Red-bellied woodpeckers are common year-round in the sandhills; also found here are wild turkey, white-tailed deer, gopher tortoise, and fox squirrel. Sandhills offer fine year-round viewing of increasingly rare southeastern kestrels.

**Directions:** *Travel north on Florida Highway 21 at Keystone Heights (about 30 miles west of Palatka). Go about six miles to park entrance on the right.*

DeLorme map 66

**Ownership:** Department of Environmental Protection (352) 473-4701
**Size:** 2,118 acres
**Closest town:** Keystone Heights

*After a winter spent in Central and South America, the summer tanager migrates to Florida in early spring. Unlike many other migratory birds which fly to breeding grounds farther north in the United States and Canada, the summer tanager nests in Florida, where it enjoys a diet of insects, particularly bees and wasps.*
ART WOLFE

NORTHEAST

## REGION THREE: EAST CENTRAL

Despite tremendous residential and urban growth, this region still preserves a variety of habitats important to wildlife.

The extensive marshes of the St. Johns River, now reduced to 65 percent of their original area, form much of the western portion of this region. Forested wetlands and marshes east of the St. Johns and Wekiva rivers are important habitat for rare snail kites, crested caracaras, many herons and egrets, bald eagles, and mottled ducks. Black bears cling to a diminishing stronghold in eastern Volusia County. Coastal resorts have burgeoned in this region, yet the beaches are still important nesting grounds for huge sea turtles. Manatees ply the intracoastal waters and springs. The salt and freshwater marshes of Merritt Island National Wildlife Refuge host 70,000 ducks and 100,000 coots each winter, and a tremendous diversity of other wildlife throughout the year.

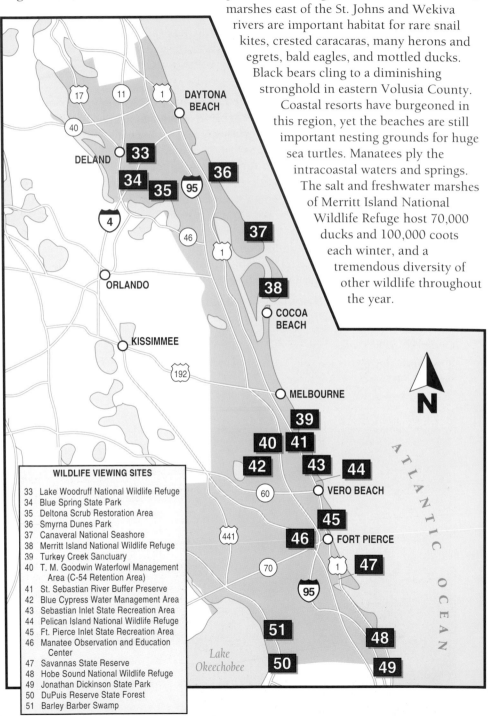

**WILDLIFE VIEWING SITES**

33  Lake Woodruff National Wildlife Refuge
34  Blue Spring State Park
35  Deltona Scrub Restoration Area
36  Smyrna Dunes Park
37  Canaveral National Seashore
38  Merritt Island National Wildlife Refuge
39  Turkey Creek Sanctuary
40  T. M. Goodwin Waterfowl Management Area (C-54 Retention Area)
41  St. Sebastian River Buffer Preserve
42  Blue Cypress Water Management Area
43  Sebastian Inlet State Recreation Area
44  Pelican Island National Wildlife Refuge
45  Ft. Pierce Inlet State Recreation Area
46  Manatee Observation and Education Center
47  Savannas State Reserve
48  Hobe Sound National Wildlife Refuge
49  Jonathan Dickinson State Park
50  DuPuis Reserve State Forest
51  Barley Barber Swamp

**Description:** This little-known refuge is comprised of 19,000 acres of freshwater marsh, swamp, and uplands bordering the St. Johns River. Miles of wide dikes surround impounded pools created to attract waterfowl and marsh birds. Two nature trails travel through pine and hardwood forests.

**Viewing Information:** October through February are ideal months to visit Lake Woodruff. Twenty-one species of waterfowl overwinter here, including ring-necked ducks, fulvous whistling ducks, and hooded mergansers. Bald eagles nest November through April. American alligators are easy to spot all year on sunny days. Sandhill cranes and most species of herons, egrets, and ibis are common. Limpkins are a special treat. Huge clouds of tree swallows roost at sunset, December through February. Wood ducks and resident songbirds begin nesting in March. Manatees move into the refuge and adjacent waters in March through November. Broods of common moorhen and rail chicks can be observed in summer. Watch for sora and king rails close to the parking area. In July and August, swallow-tailed kites are active over refuge creeks and swamps. Warbler migration, and the arrival of hundreds of vultures to roost on Tick Island are noteworthy October happenings. Year-round, river otters fish in canals and pools, and bobcat sign is often seen on the dike.

**Directions:** *From U.S. Highway 17 in DeLeon Springs, go west on Retta Street one block to Grand Avenue. Go south 0.5-mile on Grand to refuge headquarters (4490 Grand Avenue). The refuge public-use area is one mile west on Mud Lake Road.*

DeLorme map 74

**Ownership:** U.S. Fish and Wildlife Service (904) 985-4673
**Size:** 21,600 acres
**Closest town:** DeLeon Springs

*Dark brown limpkins, spotted and streaked with white, resemble the white ibis in size and shape. Look for these Florida specialties wading along river edges, and in marshes and swamps. Large freshwater apple snails are the limpkin's favorite food. The piercing cry of this bird evokes all that is wild in the southern river swamp.*

JOHN NETHERTON

EAST CENTRAL

59

**Description:** In chilly winter months, federally-listed endangered manatees leave the colder waters of the St. Johns River to take refuge in this first-magnitude spring. Fifty-five thousand gallons of water per minute flow 2,200 feet to the river through Blue Springs Run. Magnificent subtropical hardwood forest has been restored to the land surrounding the headspring. A four-mile hiking trail allows visitors to sample the habitat diversity included in this popular park. Sand pine scrub, hardwood forests with moss-draped live oaks, and seasonally-flooded swamp forests and marshes sustain abundant and diverse animal populations.

**Viewing Information:** Best chance of seeing manatees from November through March after a cold front, or other times when the temperature of the St. Johns River is below sixty-eight degrees; a boardwalk beside Blue Spring offers the best viewing. Many wading birds, including limpkin and white ibis, reside here. Look aloft for bald eagles in winter and spring, and swallow-tailed kites during early summer months. Look for scrub jays in the sand pine scrub. American alligators, river otters, and large fish often appear in the spring run, lagoon, and river mouth. *EXCELLENT MANATEE SLIDE PROGRAMS, NOVEMBER 15-MARCH 15.* Park often fills early on weekends and in summer months. Call for tour boat information. Rental cabins available.

**Directions:** *From U.S. Highway 17/92 in Orange City, drive 2.5 miles west on French Avenue to park entrance.*

DeLorme Map 80

**Ownership:** Department of Environmental Protection (904) 775-3663
**Size:** 2,600 acres
**Closest town:** Orange City

*Scrub lizards are among the rare and little-known wildlife species that reside in Florida's scrub habitat. This under-appreciated plant community is characterized by scattered oaks or sand pines, dense woody shrubs, and a blinding-white sand substrate.* JEFF RIPPLE

**Description:** This restored scrub is home to at least 200 types of plants and animals specially adapted to this fast-dwindling natural community. The hilly topography is a remnant of an ancient dune ridge that extended from Ocala to Lake Wales, formed when sea level here was much higher. Land managers are exploring a variety of management techniques in order to imitate such natural processes as succession.

**Viewing Information:** As you explore the winding trails, you will be continuously aware of the healthy population of lizards that inhabits this site, including six-lined racerunners, ground skinks, blue-tailed mole skinks, and possibly the black racer snake. Common birds in this scrub include rufous-sided towhees, red-bellied and red-headed woodpeckers, mourning and ground doves, and many small insect-eating warblers, vireos, gnatcatchers, and wrens. Watch for loggerhead shrikes perched on snags and utility lines. Keep your eyes open for Florida scrub-jays, a species managers have enticed onto this area by their restorative management practices.

**Directions:** *From Interstate 4, take Exit 53C (Saxon Boulevard). Travel east about three miles to Providence Boulevard, then north on Providence Bloulevard about three miles to Eustace Avenue and the Deltona Public Library. Turn on to Eustace; the trail begins behind the library. Self-guided tour brochures are available inside the library, at the information desk.*

DeLorme Map 80

**Ownership:** Volusia County (904) 736-5927
**Size:** 400 acres
**Closest town:** Deltona

*The loggerhead shrike is commonly called "butcher bird" because of its habit of impaling large insects, birds, mice, lizards, and other prey on plant spines or barbed wire. This black-masked hunter is often seen perched on fences or telephone wires, where it uses its excellent vision to spot prey.*

TOM VEZO

EAST CENTRAL

**Description:** At this popular park, the combination of Atlantic beach front, Ponce de Leon inlet, and the northern stretch of the Indian River often produces excellent birding. A 1.5-mile boardwalk, including an observation tower, passes through primary dunes and dredge spoil with many crossovers to the water's edge.

**Viewing Information:** From April through July, least terns and black skimmers nest here. *RESPECT POSTED AREAS; KEEP DOGS LEASHED.* Bottlenosed dolphins are commonly spotted in the inlet and ocean. During the winter months, northern gannets, common loons, and red-breasted mergansers fish close to shore. Brown pelicans, ospreys, gulls, and many shorebirds are present year-round. Great blue, tricolored, and little blue herons, and great and snowy egrets often fish along the river. From the boardwalk, look for gopher tortoise, raccoon, opossum, and beach mice. In April and October, migratory hawks, falcons, swallows, and songbirds sometimes concentrate here.

**Directions:** *From Interstate 95, take exit 84 and travel east on Florida Highway 44 to New Smyrna Beach. Cross the Intracoastal Waterway on Florida A1A and turn north on Peninsula Avenue. Proceed three miles until road ends at park entrance, adjacent to Ponce Inlet Coast Guard Station.*

DeLorme map 75

**Ownership:** Volusia County (904) 424-2935
**Size:** 250 acres
Closest town: New Smyrna Beach

*The elegant tri-colored heron, common on tidal flats and in mangrove swamps in southern and coastal Florida, is distinguished by its white underparts, white stripe down its long neck, and elongated feathers during the breeding season.* JIM ROETZEL

**Description:** Atlantic waves break on the east side of this twenty-four-mile stretch of undeveloped beach, and the waters of brackish Mosquito Lagoon lap its western edge. In between, a subtropical barrier island nurtures a diverse wildlife community with its hammocks of ancient oaks, salt marshes, mangrove islands, and tall sand dunes vegetated with sea oats, seagrape, and palmetto. Canaveral has two points of access: New Smyrna Beach to the north, and Merritt Island National Wildlife Refuge (see site 38) to the south.

**Viewing Information:** The beaches provide important summer nesting habitat for loggerhead and green sea turtles. Bottle-nosed dolphins cavort year-round in both ocean and lagoon. Manatees use Mosquito Lagoon as a refuge during spring and summer; check with the visitor center for recent sightings. American alligators are especially visible on warm winter days. Canaveral's inland waters share a tremendous population of wintering waterfowl with adjoining Merritt Island, including mottled duck, pintail, green- and blue-winged teal, American wigeon, northern shoveler, ring-necked duck, ruddy duck, lesser scaup, hooded and red-breasted merganser, and many other less commonly sighted species. Among the mangroves, watch for a variety of wading birds. Brown pelicans and ospreys are commonly observed year-round. On the beach, shorebirds are especially abundant in the cooler weather. Gulls, terns, and black skimmers are well-represented. Birding for songbirds, hawks, and falcons can be excellent during spring and fall migrations. Pleasant nature trails. Guided walks, turtle watches, and children's programs offered seasonally. *IN SUMMER, BE PREPARED FOR HEAT, INSECTS, STORMS.*

**Directions:** *See map on page 64.*

DeLorme Maps 81 and 82

**Ownership:** National Park Service (407) 267-1110
**Size:** 57,661 acres
**Closest towns:** Titusville, New Smyrna Beach

**EAST CENTRAL**

*Visitors to Canaveral National Seashore can experience the abrupt changes in natural communities as they move from the Atlantic Ocean west to Mosquito Lagoon. In less than one-half mile, wide sandy beaches change into barrier dunes, which quickly give way to subtropical mangrove trees lining the shores of the lagoon.*

JOHN NETHERTON

**Description:** One of Florida's premiere wildlife viewing areas. More than 300 bird species and fifteen federally-listed endangered or threatened species inhabit the marshes and uplands surrounding Indian River and Mosquito Lagoon. Impounded saltwater lagoons fringed by red mangroves are the principal attraction for birders. Black Point Wildlife Drive, a seven-mile dike/auto tour, is the best way to view the impoundments. The refuge shares a common boundary with Kennedy Space Center, and also adjoins Canaveral National Seashore, a twenty-five-mile beach park (see site 37).

**Viewing Information:** In November, look for such waterfowl as the northern shoveler, American wigeon, and northern pintail, as well as many shorebirds. Peregrine falcons migrate along the coast and white pelicans make their yearly appearance. Bald eagles begin to nest in late November, and red-tailed hawks, red-shouldered hawks, ospreys, merlins, and American kestrels hunt the marshes. In spring, wood storks, egrets, herons, and other wading birds court and nest. Look for Florida scrub-jays on conspicuous perches on Florida Highway 3. Shorebird migration peaks in April and again in August. Willets, sandpipers, plovers, greater and lesser yellowlegs, dunlins, and many others can be observed. Roseate spoonbills and black-necked stilts return for summer. Loggerhead sea turtles begin nesting in May, and alligators become more secretive. Insects, thunderstorms, and heat make summer visits challenging. Trails, observation tower available. Visitor center with interpretive displays, maps, and other information is open Monday through Friday 8:00 a.m. to 4:30 p.m., Saturdays 9:00 a.m. to 5:00 p.m.; open on Sundays from November through March, 9:00 a.m. to 5:00 p.m..

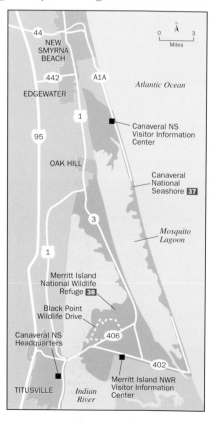

**Directions:** *See map*

DeLorme Maps 81,82,88

**Ownership:** U.S. Fish and Wildlife Service (407) 861-0667
**Size:** 140,000 acres
**Closest town:** Titusville

**Description:** Located in the heart of Palm Bay, this small sanctuary preserves a variety of habitat types increasingly rare in Brevard County. Boardwalks pass through sand pine scrub, hardwood hammock, and wet hardwood forest surrounding Turkey Creek. The creek winds through the Sanctuary, carrying its dark, tannin-stained water to the Indian River. In places, the creek cuts along the edge of the ridge of sand pine scrub; steep, sandy banks drop down over twenty feet to the river below. The hammock surrounding the creek appears lush and tropical from these high vantage points. Alligators, fish, and the occasional manatee and river otter find a quiet refuge here. A new nature center interprets the park's flora and fauna.

**Viewing Information:** The sandy soils of the sand pine scrub support gopher tortoises and eastern indigo snakes. Some common year-round residents of the dry forest include the Eastern towhee, blue jay, cardinal, raccoon, and gray squirrel. Look for the large pileated woodpecker throughout the park. The park can be accessed by canoe; launch boats at the city ramp on Bianca Drive, east of the sanctuary. The trails are open all year from 7:00 a.m. until sunset. Nature center hours are variable; call ahead.

**Directions:** *Take Interstate 95 to Palm Bay Road (exit 70A). Drive east to Babcock Street and go south to Port Malabar Road. Continue east one mile to the turn for Turkey Creek Sanctuary and the Palm Bay Library. Park in designated area.*

DeLorme Maps 88 and 96

**Ownership:** City of Palm Bay; Florida Audubon Society; Brevard County (407) 952-3433
**Size:** 113 acres
**Closest town:** Palm Bay

**EAST CENTRAL**

*The indigo snake is large and heavy-bodied with smooth, shiny-black or bluish-black scales. Although sometimes found in moist hammocks and pine flatwoods, it is most frequently encountered in dry, sandy areas where it takes refuge in the burrows of gopher tortoises. It is a Species of Special Concern in Florida because of over-collection by snake fanciers and the loss of dry habitats.*
MARESA PRYOR

**Description:** This area was purchased by the state as part of a massive commitment to restore wetlands in the upper basin of the St. Johns, Florida's longest river. The southern half of the area is divided into ten impoundments, managed intensively for migratory, wintering, and resident waterfowl, as well as wading birds and shorebirds. The northern half, a semi-permanent flooded marsh, is managed as a reservoir.

**Viewing information:** Goodwin is one of Florida's premiere areas for wintering waterfowl: expect to see the full range of dabbling duck species November through February, including blue- and green-winged teal, pintail, and American wigeon. Mottled ducks are present year-round. Swallow-tailed kites and roseate spoonbills frequent the area in the summer months. Northern harriers winter on the property, and are spotted regularly, flying low over the vegetated marshes. Visit in October to take advantage of hawk migration, when peregrine falcons, kites, and hawks hunt the area for shorebirds and other prey. White-tailed deer abound in marshes and on dikes. Quiet hikers may spot otter, bobcat, wild hog, or raccoon. Other special viewing opportunities include white and glossy ibises, bald eagles, and black-necked stilts. Call for a regulation summary, to avoid visiting during managed hunts. Area is open year-round, dawn to dusk.

***Directions:*** *See map*

DeLorme map 96

**Ownership:** Site is leased to Florida Game and Fresh Water Fish Commission (407) 726-2862
**Size:** 3,870 acres
**Closest town:** Palm Bay

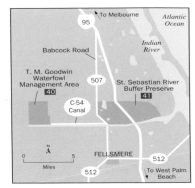

*Formerly called the marsh hawk, the northern harrier is common in Florida in all but the summer months. Its telltale white rump patch is easily visible when the bird performs its low, agile flight in search of prey over Florida's marshlands and prairies.*

TOM VEZO

**Description:** These former ranchlands were acquired by the state of Florida to protect and buffer the watershed of the Sebastian River and the Indian River Lagoon. Spacious, wildflower-filled pine flatwoods blanket much of the landscape, supporting red-cockaded woodpecker, Bachman's sparrow, Florida scrub-jay, and a suite of other rare species. The southernmost sandhill community on Florida's Atlantic coastal ridge is found here.

**Viewing information:** As many as 60 manatees congregate near the spillway of canal C-54 during the winter months and may be observed from a viewing platform at the spillway, or from the canal levee. Seasonally wet ponds and marshes are breeding sites for sandhill cranes January through June. Loggerhead shrikes, eastern bluebirds, and kestrels are commonly spotted. Bald eagles nest at several locations on the property. Call ahead to reserve primitive camping sites. The preserve is open year-round, 8 a.m. to 5 p.m.; visitor center hours vary.

***Directions:*** *See map on page 66*

DeLorme Map 96

**Ownership:** Florida Department of Environmental Protection (407) 953-5004 and St. Johns Water Management District (407) 676-6614
**Size:** 16,500 acres
**Closest town:** Fellsmere

*The cinnamon teal is a common denizen of western marshes but is a rare winter visitor to Florida. The male is distinctive with its reddish-brown plumage, but the mottled brown female is almost indistinguishable from the blue-winged teal.*
TOM VEZO

EAST CENTRAL

**Description:** West of Vero Beach and Interstate 75 lies a mosaic of wetland communities which comprise the most pristine area in the Upper St. Johns River Basin. From these marshes, lakes, and cypress swamps, the St. Johns River begins its long northward course to the Atlantic Ocean near Jacksonville. From the parking area, visitors can launch a boat to explore the marshes, bank fish, bike, or hike on levees. Many river otters live here, as well as turtles, snakes, and American alligators. This area helps support endangered snail kites and wood storks, and several wading bird rookeries. Ospreys and bald eagles hunt the area for its plentiful supply of fish.

**Viewing Information:** This site has a paved parking area, restrooms, picnic pavilions, primitive camping, and a marked canoe trail. Most visitors come to launch boats and fish. From the levee walks, look for great blue, little blue, tri-colored, and green-backed herons, white and glossy ibis, great and snowy egrets, limpkins, and anhingas. Watch for red-winged blackbirds and boat-tailed grackles in the willows and buttonbush. American coots and common moorhens are plentiful.

*Directions: Travel west about 14 miles on Florida Highway 60 from Vero Beach. Turn north onto County Road 512 and drive two miles to entrance on the left.*

DeLorme Map 96

**Ownership:** St. Johns River Water Management District (904) 329-4404
**Size:** 6,000 acres
**Closest town:** Vero Beach

*The sleek and powerful river otter uses its webbed feet and thick tail to swim with ease through streams and lakes. Otters are sociable mammals, often traveling in family groups of two or more in search of fish, frogs, crayfish, and other aquatic invertebrates.* GAIL SHUMWAY

**Description:** While this park may be famous for its outstanding surfing and fishing, its three miles of sandy beach, undeveloped mangroves, and coastal hammock appeal to the wildlife watcher as well. The park is a long, narrow barrier island, surrounded by the Atlantic Ocean and the Indian River. Sebastian Inlet bisects the park. Sea turtles nest along these beaches and shorebirds congregate on tidal mudflats. Manatees feed in the Indian River Lagoon.

**Viewing Information:** There are no nature trails in the mangroves and hammocks along the Indian River, but canoeing is delightful. There are great blue, little blue, and tricolored herons, as well as great and snowy egrets hunting for small fish and crabs among the mangrove roots. Brown pelicans and double-crested cormorants often loaf on the jetty or on exposed mudflats, along with royal terns, and ring-billed and laughing gulls. Willets, sanderlings, and dunlins feed along the beach; in fall and winter, they are joined by black-bellied plovers and ruddy turnstones. In summer, look along the beach in the early morning for the tracks of nesting sea turtles.

**Directions:** *Travel north on U.S. Highway 1 from Vero Beach to Wabasso. Turn east on Florida Highway 510 and then north for six miles on Florida A1A.*

DeLorme Map 96

**Ownership:** Department of Environmental Protection (407) 984-4852; camping reservations (561) 589-9659
**Size:** 800 acres
**Closest town:** Vero Beach/Melbourne Beach

EAST CENTRAL

*Look for single-file lines or small "V"s of double-crested cormorants near large bodies of open water, both fresh and salt. Note the orange pouch and bill of this heavy-bodied, ducklike water bird. See page 126 to compare the cormorant with the anhinga.*

MICHAEL S. SAMPLE

69

**Description:** Pelican Island, a vitally important rookery site for pelicans and 12 other species of birds (primarily storks, herons, and egrets) is a tiny, 3-acre mangrove island in the Indian Lagoon. It was designated by President Theodore Roosevelt in 1903 as the nation's first national wildlife refuge. It was set aside to protect pelicans and many related species from plume hunters. The island is accessible only by boat. To protect the birds, visitors may not disembark, and are required to keep a respectful distance.

**Viewing Information:** Birds nest on Pelican Island between late November and late July; winter is the best time to visit. Brown pelicans, wood storks, great blue, little blue and tricolored herons, white ibises, black-crowned night herons, double-crested cormorants, snowy and great egrets, and anhingas, are among the species you may view courting, nest-building, and tending to young. Watch too for sea turtles, dolphins, and manatees feeding in the Indian River. You may also view overwintering species during the cold months, including lesser scaups, blue-winged teals, mottled ducks, common loons, red-breasted mergansers, and many other species. During summer, you can expect to see roseate spoonbills, magnificent frigatebirds, and least terns.

*Directions: If you have your own boat, you may launch into refuge waters via area boat ramps. Local boat ramps may be found at the Wabasso Causeway (County Road 510); Sebastian Yacht Club on Indian River Drive in Sebastian (two blocks north of CR 512); and City Boat Ramp on Indian River Drive at Main Street and Sebastian Inlet State Recreation Area. To take a charter boat tour of the refuge, contact River Queen Cruises (561-589-6161) or Inlet Explorer (407-724-5424). Chartered cruises take about one and a half hours.*

**Ownership:** U.S. Fish and Wildlife Service (561) 589-2089
**Size:** 5,000 acres
**Closest town:** Sebastian

*The adult little blue heron has slate-blue back and wings, a bluish bill with a black tip, and bluish green legs. Immatures of this species are white and are often mistaken for snowy egrets, but careful observers will note the egret's slender black bill and black legs. The plumage of an immature is pied blue and white when changing to adult coloration.*

JIM ROETZEL

**Description:** Along the north shore of Fort Pierce Inlet, visitors can explore Atlantic beaches, dunes, coastal hammock, and mangroves. Numerous shorebirds are attracted to mudflats at low tide and butterflies find ample wildflowers to feed on. This is a popular recreation area for swimming and fishing. Birders may also want to visit nearby Jack Island State Preserve, located 1.5 miles north of the recreation area off Florida Highway A1A. The preserve is a mangrove-covered peninsula in the Indian River that attracts a variety of shore and wading birds, particularly during the winter months. Several trails criss-cross the island. A newly-constructed observation tower provides an excellent vantage point for viewing wildlife.

**Viewing Information:** From the parking area, boardwalks cross fragile dunes to the beaches. Look for gulls, terns, and shorebirds. Migrant warblers may be spotted along the nature trail in the coastal hammock northwest of the parking area. A small parking and picnic area at the southwest corner of the park provides access to Dynamite Point, a sheltered cove fringed with mangroves. There is good year-round viewing of laughing gulls, royal terns, black skimmers, brown pelicans, and double-crested cormorants. In the winter, look for semipalmated and black-bellied plovers, ruddy turnstones, willets, dunlins, and sanderlings.

*Directions: From Fort Pierce, go 3 miles north on U.S. Highway 1. Turn east on Florida Highway A1A (North Beach Causeway) and follow signs to the park.*

DeLorme map 103

**Ownership:** Department of Environmental Protection (561) 468-4007
**Size:** 340 acres
**Closest town:** Fort Pierce

EAST CENTRAL

*The black-bellied plover uses its short, stout bill to probe the mud along Florida beaches. While a few may occasionally be seen year-round, most black-bellied plovers are strictly winter residents.* BILL LEA

71

## 46 MANATEE OBSERVATION AND EDUCATION CENTER

**Description:** During the winter months, manatees seek refuge in the brackish water of Moore's Creek, where the warm-water outflow from the Fort Pierce Utilities Authority generating plant meets the waters of the Indian River Lagoon. During very cold weather, as many as 30 manatees have been spotted here at one time. Covered walkways and an observation platform facilitate viewing. Educational materials on the manatee, the ecology of the Indian River Lagoon, and the importance of habitat preservation are displayed at the visitor center.

**Viewing Information:** As with other manatee viewing areas, more of the mammals congregate in the creek when the weather is very cold. The first few days following cold fronts are usually the best. This site is directly across from the H. D. King Power Plant. THE CENTER IS OPEN FROM NOVEMBER 1 THROUGH APRIL 15 ONLY, Tuesday through Sunday, from 10:00 a.m. to 5:00 p.m.

**Directions:** *From Interstate 95 (exit 65) or the Florida Turnpike (exit 152), go east on Okeechobee Road to Virginia Avenue. Continue east on Virginia Avenue to U.S. Highway 1. Go north on US 1 to Orange Avenue. Turn east on Orange Avenue to Indian River Drive. The center is about 0.25 mile north on the right.*

DeLorme Map 103

**Ownership:** City of Fort Pierce (561) 466-1600
**Size:** N/A
**Closest Town:** Ft. Pierce

*People once thought of Florida primarily as a Disney destination, but wildlife watchers know better. More than ten wildlife or birding festivals will take place in Florida in 1998, each designed to celebrate aspects of the Sunshine State's natural biodiversity.* JEFF FOOTT

**Description:** This narrow, ten-mile-long freshwater wetland is a mix of marshes, lakes, and wet prairies—all that remains of a type of coastal wetland system once common along the southeastern Florida shore. The sand pine community on the Atlantic coastal ridge to the east is home to several rare and endangered plants and animals.

**Viewing Information:** To develop a true appreciation for this site, plan on both hiking and canoeing activities. At present, visitors must furnish their own canoes or arrange for a canoe tour as part of a private group (make reservations well in advance of anticipated visit). Look for herons, egrets, anhingas, and sandhill cranes. To hike the pine flatwoods, take the trail from Sandhill Crane Park off of Walton Road. Short spur trails afford views of the marsh. Listen for brown-headed nuthatches and pine warblers. Scan the marshes for wading birds and sandhill cranes. The Hawk's Bluff loop trail through the unique sand pine scrub community is located in a residential neighborhood off of Northeast Savanna Road (see map). Look for scrub-jays, gopher tortoises, and the fragrant wooly cactus, a rare plant found almost nowhere else but here. Future development of this site may include additional trails and canoe launch facilities.

**Directions:** *See map*

**DeLorme map:** 103

**Ownership:** Department of Environmental Protection (561) 468-3985 or (561) 340-7530

**Size:** 5,000 acres

**Closest Town:** Ft. Pierce

*EAST CENTRAL*

**Tall, graceful Florida sandhill cranes live year-round in the shallow freshwater marshes and adjacent uplands of central Florida. Their vulnerability to manmade and natural hazards makes them a state-listed threatened species.**

JIM ROETZEL

73

**Description:** Hobe Sound includes more than three miles of beach, sand dunes, and mangrove swamp on Jupiter Island, and a sand pine scrub forest on the mainland. Here, on one of the most productive sea turtle nesting areas in the United States, federally-listed endangered leatherback and green sea turtles and threatened loggerhead sea turtles crawl from the sea on June and July nights to lay their eggs. Few birds nest on the refuge, but it is extremely valuable for migratory birds. Restoration of native vegetation, and elimination of exotic Brazilian pepper and Australian pine are a major focus here.

**Viewing Information:** In winter, northern gannets, common loons, and sea ducks cruise the nearshore Atlantic waters. Walk the beach for year-round views of brown pelicans, osprey, shorebirds, and bottle-nosed dolphins. Look for endangered Florida scrub-jays, gopher tortoises, and numerous songbirds on the 0.5-mile Sand Pine Scrub Nature Trail. Seasonal interpretive programs, including summer turtle walks, are offered by the Hobe Sound Nature Center; call (407) 546-2067 for details and reservations. Refuge office, interpretive museum, and restroom facilities are located on U.S. Highway 1, one mile south of Hobe Sound. Parking is limited at the beach lot and may fill quickly on weekends.

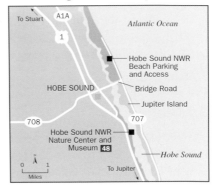

*Directions: See map*

DeLorme map 103

**Ownership:** U.S.Fish and Wildlife Service (561) 546-6141
**Size:** 968 acres
**Closest town:** Hobe Sound

*Enormous female loggerhead sea turtles emerge from the sea to nest on Florida beaches from April through July. About ninety percent of the loggerhead nests found in the United States are in Florida, with heaviest concentrations between New Smyrna Beach and Boca Raton.*

FRED WHITEHEAD

**Description:** This extensive park preserves a large and diverse portion of coastal Florida and offers a fine sampling of its many habitats. There are pine flatwoods, sand pine scrub, freshwater creeks, and cypress and mangrove wetlands along the waters of the Loxahatchee National Wild and Scenic River. Canoe, bike, and hiking trails allow many opportunities for exploration.

**Viewing Information:** Look for gopher tortoises and their burrows, snakes and lizards, and the curious Florida scrub-jay in the sand pine scrub. Woodpeckers, pine warblers, and northern bobwhite are common residents of the pine flatwoods. With luck, white-tailed deer, nesting bald eagles, wood storks, or sandhill cranes may be spotted along the main park road. Along the river, watch for ospreys, white ibises, herons, egrets, and anhingas. The self-guided Kitching Creek Trail passes through slash pine forest, and lush ferns and cypress trees bordering Kitching Creek and Wilson Creek. Another short trail near the park's entrance passes through sand pine scrub and ends at Hobe Mountain, an observation platform. The campground here may fill up in the winter. The Loxahatchee River is a popular canoeing spot and crowds may spoil wildlife viewing. Try weekdays and early mornings for more solitude. A 9.3-mile segment of the Florida Trail begins near the park entrance. Canoe and cabin rentals available; call (561) 746-1466.

*Directions: Entrance to the park is off of U.S. Highway 1, approximately seven miles north of Jupiter.*

DeLorme Maps 103 and 109

**Ownership:** Department of Environmental Protection (561) 546-2771
**Size:** 11,500 acres
**Closest town:** Jupiter

EAST CENTRAL

*Pine flatwoods are Florida's most common plant community. Slash pines and low-growing palmettos are adapted to lightning-ignited fires that burn through the flatwoods every few years. Native animals know how to avoid the low-intensity flames, and thrive on the open habitat and the fresh, tender plants that sprout after fires.* JEFF RIPPLE

**Description:** Two miles from the east shore of Lake Okeechobee, this state-owned area is a remnant of the northern tip of the Everglades. Pine flatwoods, cypress swamp, wet prairie, and marshes are being restored to their original beauty and function through reflooding, exotic vegetation control, and prescribed burning.

**Viewing Information:** White-tailed deer and wild pigs feed in open areas at dawn and dusk. Great blue, little blue, green-backed and tricolored herons, great egrets, wood storks, and white ibis frequent marshes close to the roads during the wet season. Bald eagles nest on site. One nest is easily observed through binoculars 1.2 miles south of Gate 6 on the east side of DuPuis Grade. Other eagle nests are visible from backcountry trails. Hawks, woodpeckers, and songbirds are present year-round. Vehicles allowed only on the DuPuis and Jim Lake grades; these roads may be closed periodically for maintenance or due to weather conditions. Explore four loop trails for hiking and back-packing (4.3, 6.8, 11.5, and 15.5 miles) developed by the Florida Trail Association. Most fall weekends, DuPuis is closed for hunting; call to request schedule. Horse trails also available.

*Directions: From Florida Highway 710 at Indiantown, travel six miles west on Florida 76 to Gate 2 on south side of road. Access to hiking trails is at Gate 2, horseback riding at Gate 3. Gate 1 provides access for the general public.*

DeLorme Maps 102 and 108

**Ownership:** South Florida Water Management District (561) 924-5310 in cooperation with the Florida Game and Fresh Water Fish Commission.
**Size:** 21,875 acres
**Closest town:** Indiantown

*Learn to "read the landscape" when traveling: Look for different natural communities and note the wildlife species you encounter. Note natural changes such as fire scars, as well as human impacts such as clearings or canals. With practice, you'll antici-pate the wildlife in most any area as you recognize the type and quality of habitat there.* HELEN LONGEST-SLAUGHTER

## 51 BARLEY BARBER SWAMP

**Description:** A one-mile boardwalk loops through an outstanding freshwater cypress swamp. Large bald cypress trees, red maples, and cabbage palms provide a shady canopy over a carpet of ferns, fallen logs, and aquatic vegetation.

**Viewing Information:** *ACCESS TO SITE REQUIRES RESERVATIONS AT LEAST ONE WEEK IN ADVANCE.* Drive six miles from the entrance gate to viewing area, watching for red-tailed hawks, American kestrels, belted kingfishers, and vultures, all of which are common. Deer, gray fox, bobcat, and river otter are occasionally seen. Check the banks of ditches for turtles and small alligators. Herons, wood storks, and other wading birds feed in the shallow ditches. A naturalist-led tour of the cypress swamp provides excellent interpretation of plant and animal associations. Tree trunks are resplendent with colorful lichens, orchids, and lush ferns. Listen for red-shouldered hawks, barred owls, and pileated woodpeckers.

**Directions:** *Look for a left turn to the Florida Power and Light Company's Martin Power Plant, eight miles north of Indiantown on Florida Highway 710. After crossing railroad tracks, look for a sign on the right, "Wait Here For Swamp Tours."*

DeLorme map 102

**Ownership:** Florida Power and Light Company (800) 257-9267
**Size:** 400 acres
**Closest town:** Indiantown

*Bobcats are most active at night, dawn or dusk, and are often observed hunting for rats and rabbits along such manmade travel ways as roads, paths, and fire lanes. A visitor is more likely to see bobcat sign: large accumulations of feces or small, scraped piles of earth containing feces or urine which mark their territorial boundaries.*

HELEN LONGEST-SLAUGHTER

EAST CENTRAL

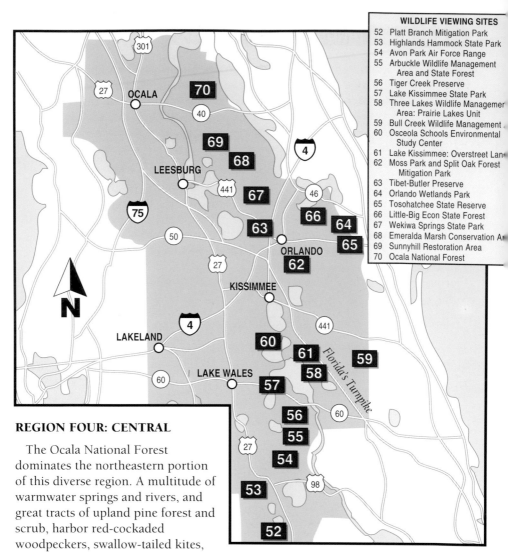

### WILDLIFE VIEWING SITES
52 Platt Branch Mitigation Park
53 Highlands Hammock State Park
54 Avon Park Air Force Range
55 Arbuckle Wildlife Management
   Area and State Forest
56 Tiger Creek Preserve
57 Lake Kissimmee State Park
58 Three Lakes Wildlife Managemen
   Area: Prairie Lakes Unit
59 Bull Creek Wildlife Management
60 Osceola Schools Environmental
   Study Center
61 Lake Kissimmee: Overstreet Lan
62 Moss Park and Split Oak Forest
   Mitigation Park
63 Tibet-Butler Preserve
64 Orlando Wetlands Park
65 Tosohatchee State Reserve
66 Little-Big Econ State Forest
67 Wekiwa Springs State Park
68 Emeralda Marsh Conservation Ar
69 Sunnyhill Restoration Area
70 Ocala National Forest

## REGION FOUR: CENTRAL

The Ocala National Forest dominates the northeastern portion of this diverse region. A multitude of warmwater springs and rivers, and great tracts of upland pine forest and scrub, harbor red-cockaded woodpeckers, swallow-tailed kites, bald eagles, scrub jays, many herons and egrets, and the black bear.

To the south is Florida's lake country. Here, among thousands of clear, natural lakes, is the greatest concentration of nesting bald eagles in the coterminous United States. The Lake Wales Ridge is home to Florida's critically-endangered ancient scrub communities. Nineteen plants unique to Florida, as well as scrub jays, sand skinks, and scrub lizards, are among the organisms diminishing as citrus groves, suburbs, and tourist facilities expand.

Two major rivers, the Oklawaha and the Kissimmee, were drastically drained and altered for flood control and agriculture earlier this century. Both are undergoing partial restoration and support important wildlife communities. West and south of the Kissimmee River, open dry prairies, pine flatwoods, and scrub and freshwater marshes support important populations of crested caracaras, burrowing owls, Florida grasshopper sparrows, snail kites, mottled ducks, and sandhill cranes. Here, too, whooping cranes are being reintroduced to Florida in the prairie region near Three Lakes Wildlife Management Area.

## 52 | PLATT BRANCH MITIGATION PARK

**Description:** Formerly a cattle ranch, this 1,710-acre park offers sweeping views of southern Florida flatwoods, along with pasture sites that are being restored to the original oak scrub vegetation. The western portion of the park includes the floodplain of Fisheating Creek, a scenic stand of oak and cypress draped with Spanish moss. The park contains high-quality examples of several rare plant communities, including oak scrub and cutthroat seeps (a fire-dependent plant community dominated by cutthroat grass, restricted to south-central Florida). Visitors can hike along an established trail system and observe a variety of endangered and threatened animal species.

**Viewing Information:** In the flatwoods, look for the cavity trees (visibly marked with a single white band) of the endangered red-cockaded woodpecker. The flatwoods also host populations of eastern bluebird, pine warbler, Bachman's sparrow, and brown-headed nuthatch. Look for the threatened Florida scrub-jay in the oak scrub vegetation. The park boasts a large gopher tortoise population, and alert viewers may see other unique species such as the sandhill crane, crested caracara, and Sherman's fox squirrel. To arrange a guided tour (for groups of 6 to 12 individuals), call the Florida Game and Fresh Water Fish Commission at (941) 465-6722. The site is in a remote location and currently lacks restrooms and other amenities.

*Directions: See map*

DeLorme Map 100

**Ownership:** Florida Game and Fresh Water Fish Commission (941) 465-6722.
**Size:** 1,710 acres
**Closest Town:** Lake Placid

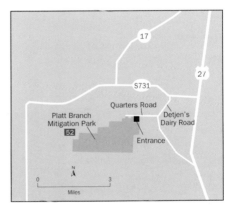

*Brown-headed nuthatches are "short-tailed acrobats," often seen spiraling headfirst down tree trunks and branches in search of insects and pine seeds. Look for their brown caps and gray backs in Florida's pine woods.*

JEFF RIPPLE

**Description:** This large, exceptionally beautiful tract was one of Florida's four original state parks. It preserves a scenic, virgin hardwood forest, a cypress swamp, and five other plant communities. Florida's last documented ivory-billed woodpecker was seen in this park. Eight short nature trails provide excellent viewing of the park's 177 bird species and other wildlife.

**Viewing Information:** Walk or ride a bike (rentals by the hour available at ranger station) along the 3.1-mile paved loop drive to see white-tailed deer, wild turkey, bobcats, pileated woodpeckers, and red-shouldered hawks. The county road is a good place to look for barred owls, American alligators, and river otters. Wading birds, including wood storks, anhingas, and little blue herons, and American alligators are frequently spotted from the cypress swamp and fern garden trails. Ask at the ranger station for a map and directions to Tiger Branch Road, a good spot to see bobcats early in the morning or at dusk. Swallow-tailed kites nest in tall pines in the picnic area and campgrounds, and glide high over the park throughout the day during spring and early summer. A ranger-led tram tour allows visitors to glimpse wildlife in remote areas of the park. Call ahead for schedule. Horse trails available.

*Directions: From U.S. Highway 27 south of Sebring, turn right on County Road 634. Travel 2.4 miles to the park entrance.*

DeLorme map 99

**Ownership:** Department of Environmental Protection (941) 386-6094
**Size:** 4,694 acres
**Closest town:** Sebring

*Freshwater swamps in Florida are usually dominated by cypress or bay trees. Many ferns, orchids, and lilies may be found here, clinging to tree trunks, on the forest floor, or growing in the canopy overhead. These wetlands provide important water storage and filtration areas, and refuge for many animals, including black bear, river otter, and swallow-tailed kite.*

HELEN LONGEST-SLAUGHTER

**Description:** Avon Park is an active military installation with generous samples of unique, endangered central Florida habitats, including dry prairie, oak and sand pine scrubs, pine flatwoods, and freshwater marshes adjoining the Kissimmee River. Public use is light at present. Birding is excellent.

**Viewing Information:** At Lake Arbuckle, a simple catwalk trail winds through lush maple-cypress swamp to an observation platform. Climb the tower for a close-up view of an active osprey nest to the north, and to observe swallow-tailed kites and short-tailed hawks over the lake. Many ducks winter here, and great blue herons, snowy and great egrets, and other wading birds forage in the marshy edges. Look for crested caracaras and grasshopper sparrows along the north side of Kissimmee Road. A walk along the Arbuckle Marsh levee may yield sightings of scores of American alligators, turtles, and most wading bird species. Red-cockaded woodpeckers, eastern bluebirds, and other flatwoods species nest on the south side of Bravo Road. A prerecorded message, updated weekly, gives more details about access (813) 452-4223. Twelve miles of the Florida National Scenic Trail parallel the Kissimmee River, transecting a band of oak hammocks which separates the river marsh from the uplands. Pileated woodpeckers, barred owls, fox squirrels, white-tailed deer, and wild turkey are frequently seen. *DUE TO MILITARY USE AND MANAGED HUNTS, SITE IS OPEN TO PUBLIC JANUARY - OCTOBER ONLY, THURSDAY NOON THROUGH MONDAY EVENING.*

**Directions:** *From Avon Park, travel ten miles east on Florida Highway 64. Stop at the natural resources office for permit, map, and other information.*

DeLorme Map 94

**Ownership:** U.S. Air Force (941) 452-4254
**Size:** 106,000 acres
**Closest town:** Avon Park

CENTRAL

*Use plumage and habitat preference to distinguish three similar Florida birds of prey: the crested caracara (this page), the bald eagle (page 84), and the osprey (page 125). Crested caracaras live only in the open rangelands north and west of Lake Okeechobee. Look for them on the ground or roadside, or perched on fence posts. Notice the black crown and crest, red facial skin, and banded tail.*
BARRY MANSELL

**Description:** This site is located on the Lake Wales Ridge, a fire-dependent scrub ecosystem that supports the highest concentration of rare and endangered plants in the continental United States. Twenty-two plant and fifteen animal species here are listed as endangered or threatened. The Arbuckle Tract of the Lake Wales Ridge State Forest encompasses the Wildlife Management Area and the Lake Arbuckle State Reserve. Lake Arbuckle, which forms this site's eastern boundary, is popular with canoeists.

**Viewing Information:** The 0.5-mile nature trail takes visitors through three primary ridge habitats: scrub, sandhills, and cutthroat seep. While all of these communities are endangered in Florida, the latter is exceptionally rare—it occurs nowhere on earth except south-central Florida. The scrub is home to rare plants such as the scrub plum and scrub blazing star, and rare animals such as the gopher tortoise, Florida scrub-jay, and sand skink (look in the sand for its S-shaped tracks). The sandhills are characterized by longleaf pine, turkey oak, and wiregrass. Brown-headed nuthatches, Bachman's sparrows, and eastern bluebirds are common. The cutthroat seep—dominated by cutthroat grass—is a moist habitat that periodically dries out. The Florida Trail meanders through the site and provides miles of excellent hiking. Exercise caution during hunting season, from mid-October to mid-November. The site is primitive and has no facilities.

**Directions:** *See map*

DeLorme Map 94

**Ownership:** Florida Division of Forestry (941) 635-7801
**Size:** 13,500 acres
**Closest town:** Frostproof

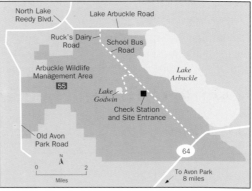

Florida's scrub lands may seem hot, dry, and uninhabitable, but they are in fact home to a diverse and unique variety of wildlife, and to more endemic and endangered plants than any other limited area in the United States. The Lake Wales Ridge Scrub and the Ocala National Forest Scrub are ancient sand dunes in Florida's central ridge. Other scrubs are found just inland of both the Atlantic and Gulf Coasts. Scrub is a threatened community in Florida because its high, well-drained lands are sought for development. Nearly 80 percent of the ancient scrub communities of central Florida have been converted to human uses.

**Description:** Like the nearby Arbuckle Wildlife Management Area and other sites on the Lake Wales sand ridge, Tiger Creek Preserve features many rare plants and animals associated with the pine and oak scrubs, pine flatwoods, hammocks, and sandhill communities. The preserve also protects the pristine Tiger Creek watershed, which flows into Lake Weohyakapka.

**Viewing Information:** Three main hiking trails (directions noted below) take visitors into the eastern and southern sections of the preserve. The George Cooley Trail is a thirty- to forty-five–minute loop trail through oak scrub, pine flatwoods, and cutthroat seeps. A short side trail goes to a hardwood swamp near Patrick Creek. The Jenkins Trail is a 1.5-mile loop that passes through a sand pine ridge before descending to the lush floodplain bordering Tiger Creek. The Pfundstein Road trails provide access to Patrick Creek (one mile from trailhead) and the longer (5.5-mile) Highlands Loop Trail. Look year-round for gopher tortoises, otters, and a variety of woodpecker species, including the striking red-headed woodpecker. The spring and summer seasons are good times to spot short-tailed hawks and swallow-tailed kites.

*Directions: For the George Cooley and Pfundstein Road trails, take State Road 17 south from Babson Park 2 miles to Murray Road. Turn left and go 2.2 miles to a left turn onto Pfundstein Road. The George Cooley trailhead is at the second power pole on the left. The nearby Highlands Loop Trail begins from a parking area located on the first left off Pfundstein Road (as you travel east beyond the Cooley trailhead). To reach the Jenkins Trail, travel nine miles east from Lake Wales on Florida Highway 60. Turn right on Walk-in-Water Road, go 3.5 miles to a right turn on Wakeford Road, and proceed to the parking area at the end of the road.*

DeLorme Map 94

**Ownership:** The Nature Conservancy (941) 678-1551
**Size:** 4,778 acres
**Closest town:** Lake Wales

*The red-bellied woodpecker is Florida's most common woodpecker. Unlike the red-headed woodpecker, with which it is sometimes confused, the red-bellied has a black-and-white barred back and red crown and/or nape. The entire head, neck, and throat are bright red in an adult woodpecker, and its solid dark back contrasts sharply with its snowy-white underparts.*

JIM ROETZEL

CENTRAL

83

**Description:** Lake Kissimmee, Florida's third-largest lake, and lakes Rosalie and Tiger nearly surround this marvelously diverse park. At least 50 species of rare animals dwell here on flowering wet prairies, expansive pine flatwoods, and dense scrub. White-tailed deer and bald eagles share the park with sandhill cranes, wild turkeys, snail kites, and burrowing owls. Periodic prescribed fires enhance the habitat for wildlife, and maintain the open vistas characteristic of central and south Florida.

**Viewing Information:** White-tailed deer, wild turkeys, and occasionally bobcats are sighted from the main road or any of the thirteen miles of hiking trails. Look for Florida scrub-jays, northern bobwhites, and eastern towhees in the scrubby flatwoods near the park entrance. Don't miss the observation tower, a great spot to scan for bald eagles and other birds of prey with a spotting scope or binoculars. Lake Kissimmee is one of the best places in Florida to see bald eagles, perhaps as many as a dozen soaring at a time. Many pairs of rare snail kites nest around Lake Kissimmee; look for them at the southern end of the lake.

**Directions:** *From Florida Highway 27 in Lake Wales, travel east on Florida 60 for ten miles to Boy Scout Road. Turn left, travel 3.7 miles, and take a right on Camp Mack Road. Proceed 5.6 miles to park entrance.*

DeLorme Maps 93 and 94

**Ownership:** Department of Environmental Protection (941) 696-1112
**Size:** 5,030 acres
**Closest town:** Lake Wales

*Unmistakable white heads and tails identify adult bald eagles, even from a great distance. More eagles nest in Florida than in any of the other lower 48 states. Tall, living pine trees near the coast or around large lakes or marshes are usual nest locations. Lake Kissimmee State Park is one of the best places in the state to observe threatened bald eagles.*

GAIL SHUMWAY

## 58 THREE LAKES WILDLIFE MANAGEMENT AREA: PRAIRIE LAKES UNIT

**Description:** Prairie Lakes lies in the midst of the highest concentration of bald eagle nesting in the contiguous United States. More than 150 active nesting territories occur around the inland lakes of Osceola and Polk counties. Kissimmee dry prairie, wet prairie, marsh, and pine flatwoods are the major habitat types on this former ranch, nestled between lakes Jackson, Kissimmee, and Marian. Frequent prescribed fires and water level restoration are returning this site to productive wildlife habitat.

**Viewing Information:** High probability of seeing bald eagles, all day, year-round. *PLEASE OBSERVE POSTED AREAS AROUND EAGLE NESTS.* Crested caracaras, sandhill cranes, northern bobwhites, red-shouldered hawks, and eastern meadowlarks are often spotted. More than 300 cavity trees of endangered red-cockaded woodpeckers are protected on surrounding portions of Three Lakes Wildlife Management Area; birds are most active at dawn and dusk. Burrowing owls are widespread but hard to see; look along elevated road berms and canal banks. White-tailed deer, wild turkey, and wild pigs are common. The Florida Trail traverses the area; other viewing is by car, bicycle, or on foot along gravel roads and unmarked trails. Obtain the WMA map and regulation summary to avoid scheduling visits during managed hunts. Primitive camping by permit only.

**Directions:** *Travel nine miles northwest from Kenansville on Florida Highway 523 (Canoe Creek Road). Entrance to Prairie Lakes Unit on left (west).*

DeLorme maps 94 and 95

**Ownership:** Florida Game and Fresh Water Fish Commission (407) 436-1818 or (352) 732-1225
**Size:** 8,203 acres
**Closest town:** Kenansville

*In south-central Florida, long-legged burrowing owls (following page) live in extensive open grassy areas, such as the rangelands of the Kissimmee Prairie. Where native habitat is scarce, they colonize vacant lots, golf courses, airports, canal dikes, and other human-altered environments.* GAIL SHUMWAY

**Description:** A remote natural area managed by the Florida Game and Fresh Water Fish Commission. Open longleaf and slash pine flatwoods, seasonally burned to promote wildlife and plant diversity, cover more than half of the area. Bull Creek, heavily forested with cypress and mixed hardwoods, meanders from south to north and eventually feeds the St. Johns River. Also present are a great variety of wetlands rich in wildflowers, including lilies, orchids, blue flag iris, yellow St. Johns wort, and pitcher plants. Begin a visit by picking up the excellent guide to the interpretive drive at the check station.

**Viewing Information:** The 8.6-mile self-guided wildlife loop drive is the best way to get to know Bull Creek. In addition, the Florida National Scenic Trail runs the length of the area. Limpkins, great egrets, green-backed and great blue herons, and white ibis stalk among the wetlands during the dry season, December through March. American alligators are visible as the creeks dry down. Sandhill cranes nest in late spring; look for them in the wet prairies, along with water pipits, common nighthawks, and marsh rabbits. Northern harriers hunt low over the prairies during winter months. White-tailed deer, wild turkey, and wild pigs frequent the oak hammocks, along with many songbird species. Gopher tortoises and their burrows are often spotted in the small scrub oak community on the west side of Loop Road near milepost 6.6. Northern bobwhite often can be seen dusting or catching insects along the wildlife drive. Call for regulation summary to avoid visiting during managed hunts.

*Directions: From Interstate 95, take exit 71 at Melbourne. At the exit ramp, turn west onto U.S. Highway 192. Travel 21.6 miles west to Crabgrass Road. Turn left and drive six miles south to the check station.*

DeLorme map 87

**Ownership:** St. Johns Water Management District; managed by the Florida Game and Fresh Water Fish Commission (352) 732-1225
**Size:** 22,206 acres
**Closest town:** Holopaw

CENTRAL

*Look for the marsh rabbit between dawn and dusk in swamps and bottomlands around the state. Though similar in size to the Eastern cottontail, the marsh rabbit has darker brown fur and lacks the conspicuous white tail.* MARESA PRYOR

**Description:** This site offers access to Reedy Creek Swamp, a twenty-five-mile-long mixed hardwood/cypress wetland, which acts as an important north-south travel corridor for regional wildlife populations. Remnant stands of ancient bald cypress trees, more than 400 years old, provide nest sites for bald eagles, red-shouldered hawks, and ospreys. Orchids, mosses, epiphytes, and ferns abound.

**Viewing Information:** From the 1800-foot elevated boardwalk, nesting bald eagles and a rookery of great blue herons are conspicuous during winter and early spring. Watch for common barred owls, red-shouldered hawks, and roosting black and turkey vultures. During dry months, flocks of white ibis and great egrets feed in full view. Flashy yellow prothonotary warblers nest in spring and summer. On sunny days, look for American alligators and aquatic turtles from the observation deck. Open to public Saturdays 10:00 a.m. to 5:00 p.m., Sundays noon to 5:00 p.m. only.

**Directions:** *From U.S. Highway 441 in Kissimmee, travel west on U.S. Highway 17/92 four miles to Poinciana Boulevard. Turn left (south) and proceed six miles to entrance on right.*

DeLorme Map 86

**Ownership:** Osceola District Schools (407) 870-0551 or (407) 870-2400
**Size:** 200 acres
**Closest town:** Kissimmee

*See if you can tell the difference between the turkey vulture and black vulture in flight. Look for the V-shaped wings of the soaring turkey vulture, pictured here. The less common black vulture (pictured on page 130) holds its broader, white-tipped wings nearly flat. Both species feed primarily on road-killed animals.* ART WOLFE

**Description:** This rustic county park offers access to and sweeping vistas of Lake Kissimmee, one of Florida's largest lakes. Here in the heart of the state's cattle country, you'll find an intriguing juxtaposition of wetland and prairie wildlife.

**Viewing information:** Along Canoe Creek and Joe Overstreet roads, be on the lookout for sandhill cranes and wild turkeys poking through the open pastures and prairies. If you are very lucky, you'll spot one of Florida's reintroduced whooping cranes, which are startlingly larger and whiter than their more common sandhill relative. Watch for crested caracaras foraging along roadsides, alone or in the company of vultures, or perching on fenceposts or in palmetto trees. Other species you might spot include bluebirds and burrowing owls. During the spring and summer months, it's not uncommon to view swallow-tailed kites dipping over the cypress strands along Canoe Creek Road. At the boat landing, settle in with a spotting scope and binoculars and watch for a dazzling display of native bird life, including glossy and white ibises, least bitterns, bald eagles, snail kites, limpkins, purple gallinules, black skimmers, and various shorebirds. As is often the case, wildlife viewing will be most rewarding early in the morning and just before sunset.

*Directions: From U.S. Highway 192 in St. Cloud, turn south on County Road 523 (Vermont Avenue), which becomes Canoe Creek Road. Travel about 20 miles, then turn right onto the unpaved Joe Overstreet Road and travel about 5.4 miles to the boat landing and small county park at the end of the road.*

DeLorme Map 94

**Ownership:** Osceola County (lease holder); site caretaker (407) 436-1966

**Size:** 5 acres

**Closest town:** St. Cloud

CENTRAL

*The state-listed endangered snail kite (formerly the Everglades kite) feeds almost exclusively on apple snails in southern and central Florida wetlands. Look for the snail kite's dark brown or slate-black back, white tail with broad dark band and paler terminal band, and slow hunting flight.*

JEFF RIPPLE

**Description:** These adjacent areas are nestled between lakes Hart and Mary Jane, about ten miles south of Orlando. Moss Park is a county-owned park with public boat ramps, campgrounds, nature trails, picnic pavilions, and other public amenities. Split Oak Forest has no facilities but offers miles of quiet hiking trails. The two areas support pine flatwoods, oak hammocks, scrub oak, sandhills, and freshwater marshes, in addition to a productive wading bird rookery at Moss Park.

**Viewing Information:** Walking trails connect the two parks, though visitors may easily drive to either's entrance. Look for wild turkeys, gopher tortoises, white-tailed deer, and Sherman's fox squirrels in upland areas. Sandhill cranes can be seen year-round. Rare whooping cranes, recently reintroduced into Florida, have been known to use this area. Look for wading birds in the wetland fringes of both lakes. At Moss Park, Bird Island (in Lake Mary Jane) supports one of Florida's top 100 nesting colonies of wading birds. Best viewing of this colony is during the early morning and evening hours, April to August. Expect to see great egrets, wood storks, great blue herons, snowy egrets, and other wading birds.

*Directions: See map*

Delorme Map 86

**Ownership:** Orange County Parks and Recreation (407) 273-2327; Florida Game and Fresh Water Fish Commission (850) 488-6661
**Size:** Moss Park: 1,550 acres; Split Oak Forest: 1,689 acres
**Closest town:** Orlando

*Controlled burns such as this one at Split Oak Forest improve wildlife habitat. Mitigation parks are important living quarters for upland species considered to be at some risk, such as gopher tortoises, Florida scrub-jays, and fox squirrels.*
JEFF RIPPLE

**Description:** This preserve offers a restful contrast to the bustle of greater Orlando, less than ten miles away. Trails meander through three major plant communities: pine flatwoods, scrub, and bayhead swamp. The preserve's Vera Carter Environmental Center houses superb interpretations of the area's natural resources, including wetlands, uplands, and fire ecology.

**Viewing Information:** The preserve's natural communities are home to a multitude of wildlife, including white-tailed deer, indigo snakes, and an array of native birds. On the Pine Loop Trail, look for gopher tortoise and other scrub specialties. Swallow-tailed kites, red-tailed hawks, ospreys, and bald eagles are often seen from the 0.5-mile Screech Owl Trail.

*Directions: From Interstate 4 West, take exit 27 (Lake Buena Vista). Go north on Florida Highway 535 (Winter Garden–Vineland Road). Travel about five miles to the preserve entrance, on the right (east) side of the road.*

DeLorme Map 85

**Ownership:** South Florida Water Management District (407) 876-6696
**Size:** 440 acres
**Closest town:** Orlando

CENTRAL

*On warm summer nights, listen for the buzzy, nasal "beep" call of common nighthawks as they forage overhead in the evening sky, or near bright lights in residential areas. This distinctive call, and their long, pointed wings, will help you distinguish nighthawks from Florida's many species of bats.*
TOM VEZO

**Description:** This park is part of an artificial wetland system designed to treat domestic wastewater. Eighteen miles of earthen berms provide easy walking or bicycling alongside cattail and bulrush marshes and open water areas studded with cabbage palm islands. Hiking trails traverse cabbage palm and hardwood hammocks adjacent to the wetland system.

**Viewing Information:** Excellent birding opportunities. In winter, open-water areas teem with waterfowl, including blue-winged and green-winged teal, northern shovelers, American wigeons, and American coots. White pelicans, glossy ibis, wood storks, black-crowned night-herons, and double-crested cormorants are also common in winter. Year-round viewing of black and turkey vultures; great blue, little blue, tricolored and green-backed herons; also great and snowy egrets, bald eagles, limpkins, and red-shouldered hawks. Hammock areas shelter woodland bird species during fall and spring migrations. American alligators and turtles inhabit the lake, with raccoons and river otters commonly seen on the berms. *SITE CLOSED DUE TO HUNTING OCTOBER 1 THROUGH JANUARY 20.* Brochure and map indicate best birding areas.

**Directions:** *Drive east of Orlando on Florida Highway 50 to Christmas, Florida. Go north 2.3 miles on Fort Christmas Road (County Road 420) and 1.5 miles east on Wheeler Road, an unpaved road. Parking area will be on left.*

DeLorme map 81

**Ownership:** City of Orlando (407) 246-2348 or 246-2288
**Size:** 1,200 acres
**Closest town:** Orlando

*Great blue herons stand motionless or stalk slowly along the shallows of many Florida waters, always on the lookout for a fish dinner. Their white heads with decorative black plumes, gray-blue bodies, and tremendous size distinguish them from little blue and tricolored herons.*

HELEN LONGEST-SLAUGHTER

**Description:** Tosohatchee preserves one of the finest examples of central Florida in its most natural state. Dirt roads and recreational trails meander through hammocks, slash pine uplands, cypress swamps, and marshlands bordering the St. Johns River. There are six active bald eagle territories in remote areas of the reserve. Hunting, fishing, off-road bicycle riding, and hiking are the most popular activities here.

**Viewing Information:** Pick up maps at the entrance kiosk on Bee Head Road. Turn left on St. Nicholas Road and then right onto the Powerline Road. Roadside ditches offer good year-round viewing of wading birds, river otters, and turtles. Look for bald eagles, ospreys, and red-shouldered hawks in open areas. Check mowed areas at dawn or dusk for white-tailed deer and wild turkey. Fox squirrels are sometimes seen in the pine flatwoods. Marshes and open water areas along the St. Johns River attract wintering waterfowl. Trailhead for the Florida Trail is at the end of St. Nicholas Road. Access to the St. Johns River is via Bee Head Road, Fish Hole Road, and Long Bluff Road, a thirteen-mile trip (oneway) on dirt roads. Scan the marshes from the Powerline Road. During seasonal hunts, wear blaze orange; call ahead for dates and regulations. Primitive camping only; reservations required two weeks in advance. Horse trails available. *NO FACILITIES.*

**Directions:** *From Florida Highway 50 in Christmas, east of Orlando, turn south on Taylor Creek Road. Park entrance is three miles on the left.*

DeLorme Maps 81 and 87

**Ownership:** Department of Environmental Protection (407) 568-1706
**Size:** 28,000 acres
**Closest town:** Orlando

CENTRAL

*The forested uplands of Tosohatchee support white-tailed deer, bobcats, turkeys, hawks, owls, and many species of songbirds. Mounds within the reserve indicate that Native Americans thrived here long before the arrival of the first Europeans—probably attracted by the same abundant wildlife we enjoy today.*

HELEN LONGEST-SLAUGHTER

## 66 LITTLE-BIG ECON STATE FOREST AND WILDLIFE MANAGEMENT AREA

**Description:** Seven miles of the Econlockhatchee River, a blackwater stream highly favored by local recreationists, winds through the heart of this property. Enjoy the new interpretive canoe trail that highlights this beautiful river system. The forest provides an essential wildlife corridor in this rapidly urbanizing part of Florida. Trails (including a portion of the Florida Trail) offer access to shady live oak hammocks, river swamp, and prairie. Primitive camping and hunting are allowed with permit; call (407) 366-8063.

**Viewing Information:** Look for large, boldly patterned fox squirrels near the Barr Street trailhead. While floating or hiking the river corridor, look aloft for swallow-tailed kites (March through July), herons and egrets (year-round), wood storks, limpkins, and bald eagles. American alligators are commonly spotted in the wetlands and the river. Sandhill cranes and northern bobwhites are year-round inhabitants of the broad pasturelands surrounding the property, and are often visible from the trails.

**Directions:** *See map*

DeLorme Map 80

**Ownership:** Florida Division of Forestry (407) 366-8063
**Size:** 4,979 acres

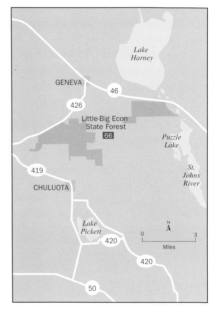

 The lovely Econlockhatchee River feeds Florida's longest and only north-flowing river, the St. Johns. The headwaters of the St. Johns are near Blue Cypress Water Management Area (site 42). The river travels north 300 miles, bulging into lakes and contracting at times into narrow, twisting water courses, on its journey to the Atlantic Ocean.

**Description:** Twenty-one miles of foot and horse trails meander through eight plant communities. Canoes may be rented to float the lovely, spring-fed Wekiwa River. Some of the finest longleaf pine sandhills in Florida survive here; Wekiwa is also a stronghold for seldom-seen black bears and many other species.

**Viewing Information:** American alligators, aquatic turtles, river otters, raccoons, limpkins, white ibis, herons, and egrets thrive along the river and its creeks and swamp. Bald eagles, ospreys, and belted kingfishers are also present. Barred owls and pileated woodpeckers are common in cabbage palm-oak hammocks near the river. In the rolling sandhills, look for fox squirrels and gopher tortoise among the longleaf pines and turkey oak. The presence of small, burrowing southeastern pocket gophers is indicated by scattered mounds of dry sand, though the animals themselves are rarely seen. Around the Sand Lake picnic area, explore the sand pine scrub community, home to a number of Florida rarities, including the Florida mouse, Florida worm-lizard, and crowned snakes. White-tailed deer are seen from the high sandhills and scrub down through the flatwoods to the hammocks and swamps. Gray fox, bobcat, raccoon, opossum, and black bear range across the entire park. Thirteen miles of trails with two backpacking campsites. *VERY POPULAR IN SUMMER AND EARLY FALL; COME EARLY TO SEE WILDLIFE.*

**Directions:** *From Interstate 4, take exit 49 and turn west onto Florida Highway 434. Go to fifth traffic light, and turn right onto Wekiwa Springs Road. Travel 4.5 miles to park entrance on right.*

DeLorme Map 80

**Ownership:** Department of Environmental Protection (407) 884-2009
**Size:** 6,900 acres
**Closest town:** Apopka

CENTRAL

*The threatened Florida black bear once ranged over all of Florida. Secure populations now exist only in the Apalachicola and Osceola national forests, and the area surrounding Big Cypress Swamp. Bears increasingly run afoul of Florida's expanding human population; many are killed in collisions with cars each year.* ART WOLFE

**Description:** Historically, the Emeralda Marsh extended for more than 10,000 acres on the eastern side of Lake Griffin, near the headwaters of the Ocklawaha River. Only 3,000 acres of the original sawgrass and wet prairie marshes remain. Emeralda Marsh was designated a National Natural Landmark in 1974. A major effort is underway to restore the floodplain ecosystems of the Ocklawaha River, and Emeralda, comprising about 6,500 acres, is part of that effort. A large and diverse suite of wildlife species is present; more than 170 bird species have been reported at the site. Emeralda is open year-round during daylight hours.

**Viewing information:** Emeralda Marsh is known for the large numbers of waterfowl that winter here, especially blue-winged teal; northern shoveler; and Florida, wood, and ring-necked ducks. Fulvous whistling ducks occur seasonally. Bald eagles occur year round, though they are most commonly sighted between September and May. Other special birds often seen include purple gallinules, limpkins, glossy and white ibises, wood storks, and most other wading birds native to Florida. The wetlands and adjacent water bodies support one of the highest alligator populations in central Florida. Bobcats and otters are occasionally spotted, often near dawn and dusk.

***Directions:*** *See map*

DeLorme Map 79

**Ownership**: St. Johns River Water Management District (904) 329-4404
**Size:** 6,500 acres
**Closest towns:** Eustis and Leesburg

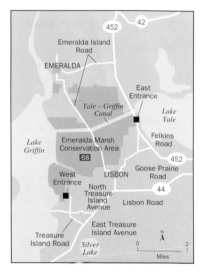

*Northern shovelers are fairly easy to pick out in a winter flock of ducks. Both males and females have a large spatulate bill, longer than the head. The adult male plumage is colorful—look for a dark green head and neck, a white breast, and rust-red sides and belly. Females are a drab mottled brown with light wing linings.*

TOM VEZO

**Description:** Nine miles of channel of the upper Oklawaha River are the centerpiece of this site. A restoration project is returning the river and its adjacent wetlands to their original function. *EXCELLENT VIEWING OPPORTUNITIES.*

**Viewing Information:** Numerous levee roads and trails offer many miles of wildlife observation. Evening counts of wading birds, including glossy and white ibis, little blue and tricolored herons, and great and snowy egrets, have been as high as 3,000 individuals. Anhingas nest in a large colony on site. Winter resident American bitterns and soras join resident king rails in the marshes. In the summer, least bitterns, black-necked stilts, and purple gallinules nest here. As many as 10,000 sandhill cranes overwinter in the Oklawaha basin, and many more may be seen flying over Sunnyhill. Resident cranes remain year-round to raise their young. Large groups of ring-necked ducks, wood ducks, and green- and blue-winged teal overwinter, along with less numerous American coots, buffleheads, northern shovelers, hooded mergansers, and northern pintails. Mottled ducks are present all year. Northern harriers winter on the property and are spotted regularly flying low over the vegetated marshes. Red-tailed and red-shouldered hawks, osprey, and three species of owls live here year-round. In summer, watch for nesting indigo buntings and blue grosbeaks. Northern bobwhite and common ground doves are often seen on the levees. Other animal species, including black bear, river otter, and bobcat have returned as restoration proceeds. Visitor center open Sundays 1:00 p.m. to 4:00 p.m. Weekday group tours by appointment. Trails open anytime; access at the "Blue House" on SR42.

**Directions:** *From Weirsdale, drive 5.9 miles east on County Road 42. Site entrance is on left (north) side of the road. Follow sign to "Blue House Information Center."*

DeLorme Maps 73 and 79

**Ownership:** St. Johns Water Management District (352) 821-1489
**Size:** 4,200 acres
**Closest town:** Weirsdale

*The glossy ibis is darkly feathered, both above and below, unlike the juvenile white ibis, with which it is sometimes confused. The ibis hunts in freshwater marshes, using its sickle-shaped bill to probe for mud-dwelling prey, especially crayfish.*
MARESA PRYOR

CENTRAL

**Description:** The deep, sandy soils of the Ocala's central ridge support the world's most extensive scrub community. Threatened scrub jays are commonly observed. Longleaf pine/turkey oak sandhills are inhabited by red-cockaded, downy, red-bellied, red-headed, and pileated woodpeckers, along with American kestrels, northern bobwhite, and wild turkey. Several hundred lakes and the forest's major springs—Alexander, Juniper Run, Silver Glen, and Salt Springs—host a great diversity of aquatic wildlife.

**Viewing Information:** Stop at one of the visitor centers for maps and bird lists. Look along Forest Road 88 north from Florida Highway 40 to see scrub jays in sand pine stands less than ten feet high. Hughes Island and Salt Springs Island are good spots to bird for sandhill species. Hopkins Prairie is an excellent place to observe Florida scrub-jays and sandhill cranes. Ospreys nest in snags surrounding the prairie. The springs draw Acadian flycatchers, prothonotary warblers, swallow-tailed kites, limpkins, and summer tanagers April through August. To see them, explore the Timucuan Nature Trail at Alexander Springs, or the Salt Springs Trail. Canoe rentals available. A great variety of fish are fascinating to watch at Salt Springs headwater. Bald eagles may be observed aloft anyplace in the forest; they are particularly numerous around Lake George.

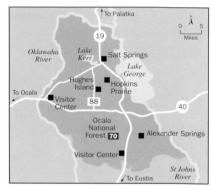

**Directions:** *See map*

DeLorme Maps 72 and 73

**Ownership:** USDA Forest Service
(352) 625-2520
**Size:** 383,000 acres
**Closest town:** Ocala

*The springs and spring runs of the Ocala National Forest, lushly vegetated with semitropical plants, offer surprising contrast to the Forest's upland sandhill and scrub communities. Canoeing is the best way to explore the beautiful spring runs and wet floodplain forests.* FRED WHITEHEAD

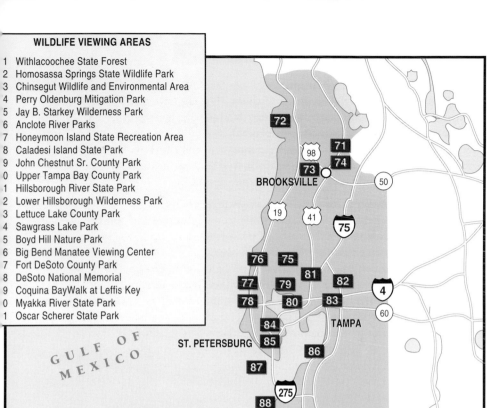

**WILDLIFE VIEWING AREAS**

1 Withlacoochee State Forest
2 Homosassa Springs State Wildlife Park
3 Chinsegut Wildlife and Environmental Area
4 Perry Oldenburg Mitigation Park
5 Jay B. Starkey Wilderness Park
6 Anclote River Parks
7 Honeymoon Island State Recreation Area
8 Caladesi Island State Park
9 John Chestnut Sr. County Park
0 Upper Tampa Bay County Park
1 Hillsborough River State Park
2 Lower Hillsborough Wilderness Park
3 Lettuce Lake County Park
4 Sawgrass Lake Park
5 Boyd Hill Nature Park
6 Big Bend Manatee Viewing Center
7 Fort DeSoto County Park
8 DeSoto National Memorial
9 Coquina BayWalk at Leffis Key
0 Myakka River State Park
1 Oscar Scherer State Park

## REGION FIVE: WEST CENTRAL

Numerous spring-fed rivers and streams traverse the northern counties in this region. The largest springs shelter great numbers of wintering manatees. Longleaf pine sandhills were historically the region's major forest type; intensely-managed pine plantations now predominate. White-tailed deer, gray squirrels, red-shouldered hawks, barred owls, woodpeckers, and songbirds live in hardwood hammock "islands" scattered among the vast pine woods.

The coastline of the Gulf of Mexico is vegetated with salt marsh to the north and mangrove forests further south, and a chain of sandy barrier islands prove hospitable to humans and wildlife alike.

Heavy urbanization has overtaken Pinellas and Hillsborough counties, and the coastal portions of Sarasota, Manatee, and south Pasco counties. Even so, stretches of wildlife habitat with excellent viewing opportunities remain in state and county parks.

DeSoto County harbors large tracts of dry prairie, scrubby flatwoods, rangeland, and sandhills. Crested caracaras, sandhill cranes, Florida burrowing owls, and mixed wading bird colonies are among the rare species found here.

**Description:** Three out of the six tracts that comprise the forest are described here (see map below). The small Headquarters Tract includes the Forestry Center and McKethan Lake. The Citrus Tract is a slightly hilly area of longleaf pine/turkey oak, sand pine and pine plantation. Habitat is similar in the Croom Tract except for cypress trees near ponds and along the Withlacoochee River. The tracts are criss-crossed with hiking trails and forest roads.

**Viewing Information:** Visit the Forestry Recreation and Visitor Center (open 8:00 a.m. to 5:00 p.m. daily) for free maps and brochures. At McKethan Lake Recreation Area, visitors may drive or walk the paved road around the lake or hike on a wooded nature trail just off the paved road. Look for typical woodland songbirds and hawks, owls, and woodpeckers in the bottomland hardwoods and pine forest along the trail. White-tailed deer may occasionally be seen near the lake at dawn or dusk. The Colonel Robins Recreation Area offers a self-guided nature trail with identification of many of the dominant trees in the pine and oak forest. Fox squirrels are common along Forest Road 13 in the Citrus tract. White-tailed deer are frequently seen here in the early evening. In the Croom Tract, drive Croom Road (Forest Road 6) through the area or visit the Silver Lake Recreation Area. White-tailed deer, rabbits, and raccoons are best viewed early or late in the day. *FOREST ROADS ARE SOMETIMES IMPASSABLE WITHOUT A FOUR-WHEEL-DRIVE VEHICLE.* Seasonal hunting may affect access.

**Directions:** *See map*

DeLorme maps 77 and 78

**Ownership:** DACS, Florida Division of Forestry (352) 754-6896
**Size:** 150,000 acres
**Closest town:** Brooksville

*Shy and increasingly rare fox squirrels usually live in dry, sandy longleaf or slash pine forests scattered throughout Florida. Notice their large body size in contrast to common gray squirrels (see page 113). Look for the fox squirrel's dark head, with varying patterns of white on the ears and nose.* GAIL SHUMWAY

**Description:** The centerpiece of this park is a large natural spring which regularly attracts at least 34 species of saltwater and freshwater fish species. The park provides refuge for captive-born and rehabilitating manatees scheduled for release back into the wild. The large windows of an underwater observatory allow visitors to view fish and manatees at close range.

**Viewing Information:** Manatees may be observed and studied in the main spring observatory. Thousands of snook, sheepshead, redfish, snapper, mullet, jack, and many other fish species frequently visit the spring. A wide variety of Florida water birds reside in the park, or migrate through, including wood ducks, egrets, herons, white ibis, and many songbirds. A large rookery of great blue herons may be observed in the park from December to June. Captive exhibits focus on native species in semi-natural habitats, including American alligators, black bear, bobcat, river otter, white-tailed deer, and waterfowl. Pontoon boats offer a scenic tour of Pepper Creek, a spring-run stream that feeds the Homosassa River. American alligators, crocodiles, manatees, and other native wildlife are the subjects of daily ranger-led programs; a Children's Education Center features hands-on exhibits.

**Directions:** *Park entrance is on U.S. Highway 19 in Homosassa Springs.*

DeLorme Map 77

**Ownership:** Department of Environmental Protection (904) 628-2311
**Size:** 177 acres
**Closest town:** Homosassa Springs

WEST CENTRAL

*Homosassa Springs is one of the only places in the world where manatees may be observed year-round at close range in a natural environment. Many species of fish are also attracted to this 32-foot-deep spring, with its comfortable and constant temperature of 72 degrees.*
DOUG PERRINE

**Description:** Chinsegut consists of two separate tracts, Big Pine (420 acres) and Chinsegut Nature Center (408 acres), both of which have served as wildlife refuges since 1932. Visitors will find sandhills, freshwater marshes and prairies, and hardwood hammocks to hike and explore on both parcels. The Big Pine tract is home to the second-largest contiguous tract of old-growth longleaf pine in Florida. The Nature Center hosts many educational programs and festivals. Call (352) 754-6722 for a list of scheduled events.

**Viewing information:** During the spring and fall months, Chinsegut is a productive site for observing migratory songbirds, including warblers, vireos, and thrushes. May's Prairie, on the Nature Center tract, is home to healthy populations of gopher frogs and barking tree frogs, dwarf sirens, and tiger salamanders, among many other amphibians, as well as a variety of herons, egrets, and ibises. Wood ducks nest on-site, and ring-necked ducks, lesser scaups, and hooded mergansers are common winter residents. On the sandhill trails, look for gopher tortoises and their burrows.

**Directions:** *See map*

DeLorme Map 77

**Ownership:** Florida Game and Fresh Water Fish Commission (352) 754-6722
**Size:** 828 acres
**Closest town:** Brooksville

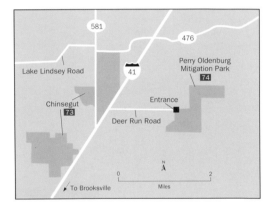

*The barking tree frog is both a high climber and a burrower. As its name implies, it has a barking call of nine or ten syllables and a single explosive "doonk" or "toonk" breeding call. It is one of the larger tree frogs and is easily identified by the profuse dark spots on its back.*

MICHAEL P. TURCO

**Description:** The rolling topography at this park is typical of the sandhill communities located along the region known as the Brooksville Ridge. The higher slopes are dominated by longleaf pine, turkey oak, and wiregrass. Oak hammocks are found in the low-lying areas, and a seasonal pond is located in the northwestern portion of the park.

**Viewing Information:** Large populations of gopher tortoises live in this park. Look around the sandy mounds at the entrances to the burrows for signs of other animals that may share underground chambers with the tortoises. These include the gopher frog, indigo and pine snakes, and the Florida mouse. This site is a good place to look for other wildlife, including fox squirrels, northern bobwhite, screech owls, and white-tailed deer.

**Directions:** *From Brooksville, take U.S. Highway 41 north 4.5 miles to Deer Run Road. Turn east (right) on Deer Run Road and go 1.5 miles to park entrance. (See map on page 102.)*

DeLorme Map 77

**Ownership:** Florida Game and Fresh Water Fish Commission (352) 754-6722
**Size:** 386 acres

*At 6 to 8 inches tall, the eastern screech owl is Florida's smallest owl. This cavity nester has a distinctive voice; a recording of its song—a long trill or "whinny"— is often used by birders to lure in warblers and other perching songbirds.*

JIM ROETZEL

WEST CENTRAL

**Description:** This large park provides a long-range water supply and passive recreation facility for Pasco County. A dozen plant communities occur on site, including pine flatwoods, sandhills, hardwood hammock, sand pine scrub, freshwater marsh, cypress and river swamp, and wet prairie. The upper reaches of the Pithlachascotee and Anclote rivers form the northwestern and southern property boundaries, respectively.

**Viewing Information:** View abundant wildlife along a 1.3 mile self-interpreted trail, eight miles of horse trails, thirteen miles of hiking trails, and a three-mile bike path, as well as the main park drive. At dawn and dusk, wild turkey and white-tailed deer are active and easy to spot along road edges. Gopher tortoises dig their burrows in the flatwoods and sandhills. Watch for eastern bluebirds, brown-headed nuthatches, and Bachman's sparrows in the flatwoods. Look for fox squirrels, too. Sandhill cranes live year-round on the wet prairies. Red-shouldered hawks, and barred and great horned owls are often heard. A bird list is available; nearly 150 species have been identified to date. *PRESERVE OPEN YEAR-ROUND, DAWN TO DUSK. NO HUNTING.*

*Directions: From U.S. Highway 19 in New Port Richey, go east on Florida Highway 54 five miles to County Road 1 (Little Road). Go north one mile on County 1 to River Crossing Boulevard. Turn right (east) and drive 1.8 miles to entrance.*

DeLorme maps 82 and 83

**Ownership:** South West Florida Water Management District; managed by Pasco County (727) 834-3247
**Size:** 8,300 acres
**Closest town:** New Port Richey

*Wild turkeys are easily recognized, but difficult to spot. They closely resemble domesticated varieties but are more slender and streamlined. In spite of their clumsy appearance, they are swift to run or fly to protective cover.* JOHN NETHERTON

**Description:** *AUTO TOUR.* This short driving loop winds along the mangrove coastline west and north of highly-developed Pinellas County. The mouth of the Anclote River and the Gulf of Mexico are accessible through two small county parks, on the south and north sides of a Florida Power Corporation electrical plant (see map below).

**Viewing Information:** Mangrove-fringed lagoons, and tidal coves and flats provide good views of many egrets, herons, and shorebirds, including wintering short-billed dowitchers and a variety of plovers; best viewing at low tide. Great blue herons nest close by. Marshes adjacent to the extensive mudflats shelter rails, white ibis, and night herons. Bald eagles nest along Bailey's Bluff Road, and are visible December through May. Ospreys also nest on site and are present year-round. Gulls, terns, and double-crested cormorants fish in nearshore waters. Look for magnificent frigatebirds high over the water, April through October. On the northern portion of the drive, watch for scrub jays in turkey oak scrub on east side of road.

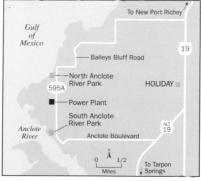

**Directions:** *See map*

DeLorme map 82

**Ownership:** Florida Power Corporation; managed by Pasco County (727) 938-2598

**Size:** Seven-mile auto tour

**Closest town:** Tarpon Springs

*Magnificent frigatebirds are regularly sighted in buoyant, graceful flight off both coasts of Florida. These huge birds with long, deeply-forked tails are unmistakable. Prey is captured in flight, including young turtles on beaches, young birds in nests, or fish on the water's surface.* JOHN GERLACH

WEST CENTRAL

**Description:** Honeymoon is a typical Gulf Coast barrier island—long and thin with white sand beaches on the Gulf side and mangrove swamps on the bay side. In between are slash pine forests and tidal flats along an interior lagoon at the island's north end. Like all the Gulf islands, Honeymoon is a good first landfall site for birds migrating across the Gulf in the spring. Nesting ospreys are common. Watch along the entrance causeway for flocks of black skimmers among the ring-billed and laughing gulls. A popular recreation area; the beach is often crowded.

**Viewing information:** The northern parking area is the trailhead for two nature trails which traverse undeveloped portions of the island. Both are good for observing nesting ospreys and migratory warblers. The Pelican Cove Trail passes along the edge of a sheltered lagoon which is often good for views of great and snowy egrets, tricolored, little blue, and great blue herons. Reddish egrets are occasionally seen. Shorebirds, including whimbrels, godwits, and dowitchers, are common. Threatened least terns nest here. *RESPECT POSTED SHOREBIRD NESTING AREAS.*

**Directions:** *About three miles north of Dunedin, turn west on Curlew Road (Florida Highway 586) from U.S. Highway 19 or Alternate 19. Follow signs to park entrance.*

DeLorme map 82

**Ownership:** Department of Environmental Protection (727) 469-5942
**Size:** 407 acres upland, 1800 acres submerged
**Closest town:** Dunedin

*The least tern is easy to identify with its snow-white forehead, black crown, and bright yellow bill and legs. Watch for this tiny, graceful tern plunge-diving into shallow coastal waters in search of small fish. In Florida, human disturbance has driven many least terns from their traditional nesting beaches. Most least tern nesting colonies are now located on spoil islands or rooftops.* BARRY MANSELL

**Description:** Until the hurricane of 1848, Caladesi Island was a part of Honeymoon Island, its neighbor to the north. The beaches, mangroves, slash pine uplands, and maritime hammock communities are similar, but Caladesi is isolated from the mainland and undeveloped. Visitors reach the island by ferry or private boat. Walks along sand beach or a nature trail through the island's interior offer a respite from the coast's commercial development.

**Viewing Information:** Walk the shoreline and look for bottle-nosed dolphins offshore, or crawl marks left by loggerhead turtles coming ashore during the night to lay their eggs, May through September. Gulls, terns, and shorebirds patrol the beach and exposed sandbars, particularly on the south end of the island. Herons, egrets, and other wading birds often feed in the shallow water in mangrove areas behind the dunes. A self-guided nature trail explores the island's interior and is well-interpreted in a free park brochure. Look for tracks of raccoons, gopher tortoises, and snakes in sand along the trail. Interior woods attract migratory warblers in spring and fall. *ISLAND ACCESSIBLE BY PASSENGER FERRY OR PRIVATE BOAT ONLY.* Commercial ferry departs from Honeymoon Island State Recreation Area and Clearwater. Call ahead for schedule information (813-734-5263). Bayside marina for private boat.

**Directions:** *To reach ferry dock on Honeymoon Island, travel west on Curlew Road (Florida Highway 586) from U.S. Highway 19 or Alternate 19 in Dunedin. Follow signs to park entrance.*

DeLorme map 82

**Ownership:** Department of Environmental Protection (727) 469-5918 or (727) 469-5942
**Size:** 630 acres upland, 1800 acres submerged
**Closest town:** Dunedin

*This hatchling leatherback sea turtle has just emerged from its beachfront nest with a group of its siblings and is scrambling to the sea. The young apparently find the ocean by moving towards the bright, open horizon. Many predators await the young turtles; only a few will survive to maturity.*

DOUG PERRINE

WEST CENTRAL

**Description:** This park preserves cypress swamps and pine flatwoods on the southeastern shore of large Lake Tarpon. Nature trails are lush and shady, and Brooker Creek at the south end of the park makes for quiet and pleasant canoeing. Boaters may access the park from the lake. Bald eagles and ospreys are easy to spot, while limpkins are sometimes observed daintily making their way through shoreline vegetation in search of apple snails. The park has nice picnic and playground facilities and is a popular recreation spot.

**Viewing Information:** The self-guided Peggy Park Nature Trail provides excellent interpretation. The slash pines, oaks, and palmettos at the start of the trail grade into a moist, shaded cypress swamp. Ferns form a dense ground cover beneath a canopy of cypress and red maple. At the lake's edge, look for snakes, turtles, and American alligators sunning themselves on logs and exposed roots. Woodpeckers, red-shouldered hawks, and barred owls are common in the swamp—often heard rather than seen. The lookout platform on the nature trail in the north end of the park is a likely spot to observe ospreys and bald eagles flying over Lake Tarpon.

**Directions:** *From U.S. Highway 19 in Palm Harbor, go east on Tampa Road (Florida Highway 584) to East Lake Road. Go north two miles to entrance on left.*

DeLorme Map 82

**Ownership:** Pinellas County (727) 784-4686
**Size:** 255 acres
**Closest town:** Palm Harbor

*With the extirpation of the ivory-billed woodpecker from the old-growth swamps of North America, the pileated woodpecker is the largest of the four remaining woodpecker species seen year-round in Florida. It is conspicuous by its size, black and white plumage, and large red crest.*

GAIL SHUMWAY

**Description:** This park stands as an excellent example of how the coastal wetlands in this area looked prior to urbanization. Salt marshes, mangroves, slash pine uplands, and salt barrens are surrounded by Old Tampa Bay and Double Branch Creek. Good canoeing.

**Viewing Information:** Visit the outstanding nature center for an overview of the park's history and ecology. Several nature trails and boardwalks simplify the exploration of otherwise inaccessible salt marsh and mangrove wetlands. Herons, egrets, terns, white ibis, brown pelicans, northern harriers, and ospreys are common. On the Otter Trail through pine flatwoods, look for rufous-sided towhees, gray catbirds, songbirds, and the occasional rattlesnake.

*Directions: From Oldsmar, travel about two miles southeast on Hillsborough Road (Florida Highway 580). Turn south onto Double Branch Road and drive 0.5-mile to park entrance.*

DeLorme map 83

**Ownership:** Hillsborough County (727) 855-1765
**Size:** 2,144 acres
**Closest town:** Oldsmar

The Eastern diamondback rattlesnake is the largest of Florida's poisonous snakes and is found throughout the state. Harassment and encroaching development continue to cause population declines. This snake's large reserve of venom and tremendous striking speed demand extreme caution on the part of wildlife viewers—in fact, it's best to simply leave this animal alone. JOHN NETHERTON

WEST CENTRAL

81  HILLSBOROUGH RIVER STATE PARK

**Description:** The picturesque Hillsborough River flows through 2,994 acres of live oak hammock, cypress swamps, pine flatwoods, and freshwater marshes in one of Florida's oldest parks. Eight miles of nature trails give visitors a chance to escape the crowds and glimpse beautiful native habitats and their associated wildlife.

**Viewing Information:** This park is close to Tampa and is a popular destination for recreationists. Early morning hikes on one of three brief trails, or a longer excursion on the 3.4-mile Florida Trail loop (on the north side of the river) yield the greatest chance of catching glimpses of wildlife. Visitors wishing to hike the Florida Trail loop should register with the office and carry drinking water. Typical wildlife species include fox, raccoon, striped skunk, bobcat, deer, and migratory warblers. Look for otters, alligators, turtles, and snakes in or along the river. Signs of feral hog and armadillo are common. Note: Swimming is permitted in the artificial swimming area only—not in the river. Canoe rentals are available.

*Directions: Take Interstate 75 to exit 54 (Florida Highway 582). Go east on Florida 582 for one mile to U.S. Highway 301. Travel east on US 301 for 9 miles to park entrance.*

DeLorme Map 83

**Ownership:** Department of Environmental Protection (813) 987-6771
**Size:** 2,994 acres
**Closest Town:** Thonotosassa

*Like other green frogs, the green tree frog is a great climber and is often seen clinging to Florida windows at night hoping to get at the insects attracted by our living room lights. The frogs use the sticky pads on their toes to hold themselves close to the light source and the many insects attracted to it. Most individuals of this species are bright green, but colors may vary from yellow to a dull greenish or slate gray.*

JEFF RIPPLE

110

**Description:** This site is a regional park with five separate recreation sites providing access to the creeks and floodplain forest surrounding the Hillsborough River. All sites are designed for canoeing, hiking, or bicycling. Of the five sites, four lend themselves well to wildlife viewing. One is an upland site and three have boardwalks through wetlands, along with canoe launch facilities. Canoe rentals are available from private concessions in Thonotosassa. All sites are barrier-free. No swimming, due to pollution from agricultural sources.

**Viewing Information:** The canoeing sites include Trout Creek Park, Morris Bridge Park, and John B. Sargeant Memorial Park. All three have restrooms, boardwalks, canoe launches, and picnic and fishing areas. From a canoe, wading birds such as great blue, little blue, and green-backed herons, great egrets, white ibis, and limpkins may be seen. Look for turtles and American alligators on riverbanks and fallen logs. White-tailed deer, wild turkeys, and wild pigs are occasionally seen near the water's edge. The Flatwoods site offers a nine-mile bicycling, jogging, or skating route through pine flatwoods. Quiet canoeists may surprise a river otter.

**Directions:** *See map*

DeLorme map 83

**Ownership:** Southwest Florida Water Management District; managed by Hillsborough County: Flatwoods Park (813) 987-6211, Morris Bridge (813) 987 6209, Trout Creek Park (813) 987-6200, John B. Sargeant Memorial Park (813) 987-6208.

**Size:** 15,897 acres

**Closest town:** Tampa

The red-shouldered hawk is stocky, with a mottled brown-and-white back and wings. Look for its dark tail with three narrow white bands, and the finely-barred breast feathers. These hawks are common residents of Florida wetlands; watch for them perched in trees, scanning the ground for mice, marsh rabbits, snakes, and other prey.
MICHAEL S. SAMPLE

WEST CENTRAL

111

**Description:** This "lake" is actually a shallow, fingerlike portion of the Hillsborough River, whose tributaries and broad floodplain lie northeast of Tampa. A tall observation tower stands at the junction of Lettuce Lake and the river and overlooks hardwood swamp. Numerous birds and reptiles are attracted to the shallow waters of Lettuce Lake, including wood ducks, American alligators, and wading birds. From the 3,500-foot-long boardwalk through the swamp, listen for woodpeckers and barred owls. This area attracts migratory warblers and is a good place to see the prothonotary warbler, a bright yellow summer visitor. An upland nature trail, cypress swamp with short boardwalk, a pedestrian/bicycle path, visitor center, and picnic and play field facilities attract many visitors.

**Viewing Information:** This park is very popular for group activities and becomes quite crowded; for best viewing, come early in the day when the park is quiet and birds are actively feeding. From the boardwalk and observation tower along Lettuce Lake, look for great blue, little blue, green-backed, and tricolored herons, great and snowy egrets, white ibis, and wood ducks. American alligators and turtles are common. The tower and boardwalk close one half hour before the park.

*Directions: On Interstate 75, just west of Tampa, take exit 54. Travel west 0.9 mile on Fletcher Avenue to park on north side of road.*

DeLorme map 83

**Ownership:** Hillsborough County (813) 987-6204
**Size:** 240 acres
**Closest town:** Temple Terrace

*The wood duck is one of only two duck species that reside year-round in Florida. They often feed on the ground in cypress swamps and floodplain forests. Acorns are a dietary mainstay for this beautiful bird. The female is at left above; male at right.*

JOE MAC HUDSPETH

**Description:** Within the heart of urbanized Pinellas County, this park serves a dual function. Its lake, maple swamp and manmade canals act as a water retention site to help prevent flood damage. These same features attract wildlife and provide an opportunity for public education. A mile of elevated boardwalk winds through a maple swamp and oak hammock. An overlook tower at Sawgrass Lake provides good views of herons, egrets, white ibis, common moorhens, and red-winged blackbirds.

**Viewing Information:** Visitors should first stop at the Anderson Environmental Center. A large freshwater aquarium and other exhibits provide some background on the geologic, biological, and cultural forces that shaped the park and surrounding region. A detailed booklet guides the visitor on an ecological tour of the park. From the overlook tower, scan the lake for great blue, little blue, tricolored and green-backed herons, great and snowy egrets, white ibis, and common moorhens. Limpkins may be seen hunting the lake's edge. Look for turtles, American alligators, and snakes on exposed logs and roots. Gray squirrels are numerous and very bold.

**Directions:** *See map*

DeLorme map 90

**Ownership:** Southwest Florida Water Management District; managed by Pinellas County Parks Department, (727) 527-3814
**Size:** 390 acres
**Closest town:** St. Petersburg

WEST CENTRAL

*The bushy-tailed gray squirrel is a familiar sight in most Florida parks. Its charming poses invite handouts, but it is best left to forage for its natural diet of nuts and fruits. Many of the seeds and fruits are buried in shallow holes, where some will sprout and naturally contribute to reforestation.* BILL LEA

**Description:** Situated in the midst of a growing city of a quarter of a million people, Boyd Hill has much to offer the wildlife observer or student of nature. Three miles of trails and boardwalks lead visitors through hardwood hammock, sand pine scrub, pine flatwoods, willow marshes, and lake shore.

**Viewing Information:** Great blue herons, snowy egrets, and black-crowned night herons are among the wading birds frequently seen in Boyd Hill's wetlands. The Willow Marsh Trail is a good place to spot American alligators, frogs, aquatic turtles, American coots, and common moorhens. Look aloft for magnificent frigatebirds, wood storks, ospreys, and bald eagles while strolling among the mangroves adjoining Lake Maggiore. Mottled ducks and pied-billed grebes are present on the lake year-round; ring-necked ducks and scaup occur in the fall and winter. The Scrub Island Trail, in the center of the property, hosts threatened species such as gopher tortoise, and indigo snakes. In the early morning, walk the Pine Flatwoods Trail to view fox squirrels, raccoons, Virginia opossum, and a variety of birds, including northern bobwhite and rufous-sided towhee. All trails are accessible by foot and bicycle. The nature center features four large aquaria with native fish, an observation beehive, and many display cases interpreting local fauna and flora. The park is open from 9:00 a.m. to 5:00 p.m. daily; 9:00 a.m. to 8:00 p.m. on Tuesdays and Thursdays, April to October. Good barrier-free access.

*Directions: In St. Petersburg, from Interstate 275, take exit 4 (54th Avenue South). Travel east on 54th Avenue South to 9th Street. Turn left and head north to Country Club Way South; nature center is on right. Enter Gate 2.*

DeLorme map 90

**Size:** 800 acres
**Ownership:** City of St. Petersburg (727) 893-7326
**Closest town:** St. Petersburg

*Common moorhens are chickenlike birds often seen on freshwater lakes and marshes. The bright yellow-tipped, red bill and frontal shield are characteristic field marks.*

MARESA PRYOR

114

**Description:** Manatees find winter refuge here in the warm-water discharge canal of Tampa Electric Company's generating plant on Tampa Bay. As many as 120 of these aquatic mammals have been spotted at one time in the canal during very cold weather. The site was designated a state manatee sanctuary in 1986. A new environmental education building has exhibits on the manatee and its habitat. A platform over the shallow canal provides excellent views of manatees and large fish such as tarpon, catfish, snook, and mullet. Another boardwalk passes through mangroves alongside the canal. Look for fiddler crabs and other wildlife among the mangrove roots.

**Viewing Information:** Generally, there are more manatees in the canal when the weather is very cold. Days following cold fronts are the best. This site is directly across from Tampa Electric's largest power plant, Big Bend Station. *SITE OPEN MID-NOVEMBER THROUGH THE FIRST WEEKEND IN APRIL,* daily 10:00 a.m. to 5:00 p.m. Closed Thanksgiving Day, Christmas Day, and Easter Sunday.

**Directions:** *Take Interstate 75 to Apollo Beach (exit 47). Turn west on Big Bend Road. Proceed through the traffic light at U.S. Highway 41 to park entrance at the corner of Dickman and Big Bend Roads.*

DeLorme map 91

**Ownership:** Tampa Electric Company (813) 228-4289
**Closest town:** Apollo Beach

WEST CENTRAL

*The United States population of endangered West Indian manatees—approximately 1,200 animals—is concentrated primarily in Florida. Manatees (following page) move freely around Florida's rivers, springs, and coastal waters. Unfortunately, human activities, including pollution and habitat loss, harassment, and boat or barge hits, seriously threaten this gentle plant-eater. Between November and March, large numbers of manatees converge at sources of warm water. Crystal River, Blue Spring, Everglades National Park, and several power plants all host aggregations of manatees when the air temperature goes below 50 degrees F, and the water temperature dips below 70-72 degrees.* JEFF FOOTT

**Description:** A stellar birding spot, Fort DeSoto attracts birders from across the country who come to view spring migrants. The park is located on Mullet Key, an island that juts out into the Gulf of Mexico and Tampa Bay, south of St. Petersburg. Access to the island is via toll bridge. There are beaches, mangroves, and hardwood hammock. This is a very popular recreation area.

**Viewing Information:** A free checklist of birds, along with a map and list of the 12 best birding sites, is available at the visitor center. Scan the narrow shoreline along both sides of Florida Highway 679 near the park entrance for good year-round viewing of brown pelicans, double-crested cormorants, herons, egrets, white ibis, plovers, gulls, terns, and black skimmers. Because it is the first landfall for many songbirds returning to North America across the Gulf of Mexico each spring, the park sometimes concentrates large numbers of birds. The greatest influx of migratory warblers occurs here between early March and mid-May. Viewing is particularly good in the trees east of the fishing pier parking lot and in the woods at the Arrowhead Family Picnic Area. Look for tracks of sea turtles along the beaches in the summer.

**Directions:** *In St. Petersburg, from US Highway 19 or Interstate 275, go west on the Pinellas Bayway (54th Avenue South or Florida Highway 682), turn south on Florida 679 and follow signs to park.*

DeLorme map 90

**Ownership:** Pinellas County (727) 866-2484
**Size:** 900 acres
**Closest town:** St. Petersburg

WEST CENTRAL

*Fort DeSoto is of most interest to birders and photographers during spring and fall migration. Recreationists come to the park to go fishing and clamming, and to swim and shell on the park's beautiful beaches.* HELEN LONGEST-SLAUGHTER

**Description:** This small site near the mouth of the Manatee River preserves rich ecological and historical resources associated with the mangrove wetlands identified as De Soto's 1539 winter encampment. A short nature trail explores the mangrove swamp.

**Viewing Information:** The 0.5-mile, self-guided trail provides good interpretation of the plant and animal life associated with the semi-tropical Florida Gulf coast. Best viewing times are dawn and dusk. Look for raccoons as they forage for crabs and small fish in the mangroves. Porpoises are common in Tampa Bay. Check beach and shallow waters for wading birds such as great and little blue herons, great and snowy egrets, and willets and other shorebirds. Yellow-crowned night herons are sometimes spotted in the mangroves. Near the parking area, check the live oaks for migratory warblers in spring and fall. Anoles and skinks are plentiful on the trails. The site is open year-round, sunrise to sunset. The visitor center is open 9 a.m. to 5 p.m. every day except Thanksgiving, Christmas, and New Year's Day.

*Directions: Head west from downtown Bradenton on Florida Highway 64 for approximately five miles. Turn north (right) on 75th Street West and travel 2.5 miles to park entrance.*

DeLorme Map 90

**Ownership:** National Park Service (941) 792-0458
**Size:** 25 acres
**Closest Town:** Bradenton

*The great-crested flycatcher's call is distinctive—a loud, whistled "zweep, zweep." It breeds statewide, but migrates south in the winter to southern Florida, Mexico, and South America. Look for this flycatcher's yellow belly, cinnamon-rufous tail, and olive-brown back and crest.*

TOM VEZO

**Description:** The Baywalk is part of a larger program to restore portions of the mangrove-forested shoreline of Sarasota Bay. Only twenty percent of this vital and productive habitat for marine life and wading birds still remains. At this site, dredge spoil and non-native vegetation have been removed and tidal lagoons have been recreated. Bird and marine life is abundant.

**Viewing Information:** From the footpaths and boardwalks, observe a wide variety of bay organisms. Tidal lagoons are a favorite feeding ground for great white, little blue, and tricolored herons, black-crowned and yellow-crowned night herons, snowy egrets, and glossy and white ibis. In the lagoons, visitors may also see blue crabs, whelks, conchs, ragged sea hares, and many kinds of small fish, including juvenile mullet, black drum, redfish, snook, fan-tailed mollies, and killifish. Fiddler crabs are plentiful at low tide. During April and October, the boardwalks and center hill can be great spots to observe migrating hawks. Look for osprey and brown pelicans year-round; magnificent frigatebirds in the summer. Gulls and terns are common aloft and offshore from the beach.

**Directions:** *From Interstate 75 in Bradenton, take exit 42 and drive west 13 miles on Florida Highway 64 to Anna Maria Island. Drive south 3.5 miles on Gulf of Mexico Drive (Florida 789). Site entrance is on left (east) side of road.*

DeLorme maps 90 and 96

**Ownership:** Manatee County (941) 359-5841
**Size:** 30 acres
**Closest town:** Bradenton Beach

WEST CENTRAL

*The delicately hued blue crab is commonly encountered in shallow bays and estuaries around the state. Many species of saltwater fish consume the crab in its larval and juvenile stages. Harvest of adult blue crabs supports the third-largest commercial fishery in Florida.* FRED WHITEHEAD

**Description:** Florida's largest state park is known for its scenic vistas and abundant wildlife. It includes one of the largest tracts of dry prairie habitat in southwest Florida, Sarasota County's two largest lakes, extensive river marsh, and twelve miles of the Wild and Scenic Myakka River. Easy wildlife viewing is possible along the seven-mile park drive. Watch for white-tailed deer, raccoons, wild turkey, and more than 200 bird species. Managers are removing non-native plants and animals, and using prescribed burning to maintain and restore wildlife habitats on site.

**Viewing Information:** The park's large alligators bask year-round at midday, along the marshy edges of lakes and wetlands. The Bird Walk, 1.5 miles south of Clay Gully Picnic Area on North Park Drive, is a good place to look for abundant resident wading birds, including white ibis, great and little blue herons, great and snowy egrets, limpkins, and tricolored herons. Wintering waterfowl common on Myakka lakes include American wigeon, northern pintail, green and blue-winged teal, and ring-necked ducks. Wood ducks may be spotted year-round. Sandhill cranes and bald eagles are most visible late fall through spring. Watch for osprey and red-shouldered hawks aloft all year. Thirty-nine miles of backcountry trails available for hikers. Interpretive center. Wildlife and nature tours by tram and boat offered on a seasonal basis; call for details. Canoe and cabin rentals available.

**Directions:** *Just south of Sarasota, on Interstate 75, take exit 37. Travel east on Florida Highway 72 nine miles to park entrance.*

DeLorme map 97

**Ownership:** Department of Environmental Protection (941) 361-6511
**Size:** 28,876 acres

The Myakka River, with its abundant wildlife and fish, has been important to the people of Florida for at least 10,000 years. In 1985, the 34-mile portion of the river within Sarasota County was designated a state Wild and Scenic River. Wildlife viewers can enjoy the 12 miles of river flowing through the Myakka River State Park by renting a canoe at the park's concession.

HELEN LONGEST-SLAUGHTER

**Description:** Pine flatwoods and scrubby flatwoods, both important habitats for a number of declining species in Florida, are protected in this park. Scrub-jays, gopher tortoises, gopher frogs, and indigo snakes benefit from active management and restoration, including prescribed burning.

**Viewing Information:** One of the best locations in west Florida to see scrub jays. Park at the north side of Lake Osprey and walk into the scrubby flatwoods to the northwest. Family groups of curious Florida scrub-jays often come close to visitors on their own. *DO NOT FEED THE BIRDS.* Look for gopher tortoises and their burrows in this scrub habitat. From October to May, bald eagles nest here and are commonly spotted overhead throughout the park. Rent a canoe and float down lovely, tidal South Creek. In its marshes, mangroves and estuary, look for herons, egrets, and rails. Warblers and woodpeckers inhabit several hundred acres of pine flatwoods in this park.

***Directions:*** *Travel two miles south of Osprey on U.S. Highway 41 to park entrance on left.*

DeLorme map 97

**Ownership:** Department of Environmental Protection (941) 483-5956
**Size:** 1,383 acres
**Closest town:** Osprey

WEST CENTRAL

*Beautiful, threatened scrub-jays are easily distinguished from much more common blue jays: they have no crest, and their feathers are a lighter, sky blue. These curious animals live only in the dry oak scrub habitat of central Florida. Spreading development and agriculture have greatly reduced their numbers. Look for scrub-jays at sites 31, 35, 38, 41, 48, 49, 52, 55, 57, 70, and 91 in this guide. And don't feed them!*
MARESA PRYOR

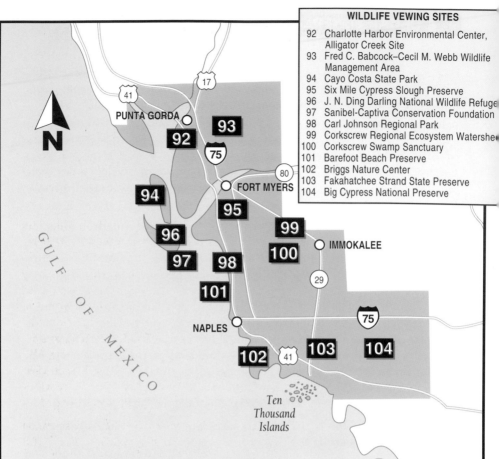

## REGION SIX: SOUTHWEST

The northern inland reaches of this region
are dominated by seasonally-flooded pine
flatwoods dotted with small ponds. To the south
the land/water balance shifts, and the landscape is
more and more inundated with very shallow water
moving slowly to Florida Bay. Major habitats include
pine flatwoods, oak and cabbage palm hammocks, sand
pine scrub, cypress domes, and dry prairies.

The vast wetlands and forests of such preserves as Big
Cypress, Fakahatchee Strand, and the western Everglades form  the
heart of remaining habitat for highly endangered Florida panthers.

The coast is rapidly developing from Port Charlotte south to Naples. Barrier
islands trace the coast as far south as Marco Island. Productive mangrove-
lined bays and estuaries with rich seagrass bottoms nurture many saltwater
species, and support nesting wading birds, ospreys, and bald eagles. Manatees
frequent the coastal rivers and the Ten Thousand Islands.

Conversion of natural lands to citrus groves and residential housing is a
serious threat to wildlife populations in this region.

**Description:** The center is located on 3,000 acres of diverse habitat bordered on the north by Alligator Creek, and on the west by Charlotte Harbor. A one-mile trail meets the creek, and traverses pine-palmetto flatwoods, cabbage palm and oak hammock, fresh and saltwater marsh, and mangrove swamp. On a longer 1.75-mile trail, visitors hike through flatwoods, beautiful stands of old cabbage palms, a brackish pond, and oak hammock. Stop at the visitor's reception building to view an exhibit of area ecosystems and beautiful carved wood replicas of birds and fish. A touch tank, mounts of local birds, and fossils can be seen in a small museum annex.

**Viewing information:** On sunny winter days, watch for American alligators basking in ponds and other wetlands. Softshell and other aquatic turtles are also common. Gopher tortoises and their sandy, excavated burrows are frequently seen in the flatwoods. Snakes, including the rare eastern indigo, may be spotted on the trails year-round. From December through April, watch for nesting bald eagles. In spring, migratory warblers are frequently observed in the hammocks. Bobcat are active year-round in the early morning. Note the black vulture roost on the long trail. Woodpeckers, including pileated, are active in the flatwoods all year. Look for a variety of herons and egrets along Alligator Creek and in the marshes. Center is open Monday through Saturday, 8:00 a.m. to 3:00 p.m. Summer hours (Memorial Day to Labor Day) are Monday through Saturday, 8:00 a.m. to noon. Photographer's blind available.

**Directions:** *From U.S. Highway 41 southeast of Punta Gorda, turn south on Burnt Store Road (Florida Highway 765). Travel one mile; entrance is on west side of road.*

DeLorme map 104

**Ownership:** Department of Environmental Protection; managed by Charlotte Harbor Environmental Center, Inc. (941) 575-5435
**Size:** 3000 acres
**Closest town:** Punta Gorda

*Softshell turtles are common in Florida's lakes and ponds; their soft and leathery shells resemble the muddy substrates where they like to bury themselves. From these shallow-water retreats, they can extend their long necks and take in a breath of fresh air at the water's surface.*

SOUTHWEST

## 93 FRED C. BABCOCK–CECIL M. WEBB WILDLIFE MANAGEMENT AREA

**Description:** Open stands of slash pine flatwoods and seasonally flooded, wildflower-rich prairies and marshes dominate the Webb. This area probably looks very much as it did prior to European settlement. Controlled fires are used every year to suppress woody, perennial vegetation and enhance the growth of grasses and other foods favored by northern bobwhite, the Webb's key species. Water levels are controlled and non-native vegetation is removed to improve conditions for wading birds and other aquatic species.

**Viewing Information:** At dawn and dusk, northern bobwhite, rabbits, gray squirrels, and raccoon are most active in the pine flatwoods. Occasional white-tailed deer move at this time of day as well. Twenty-seven colonies of federally-listed endangered red-cockaded woodpeckers occur on the Webb; look for nest trees marked with a white painted ring. Family groups of this small, black-and-white woodpecker can often be seen and heard near their cavity trees early in the morning or just before nightfall. Bald eagles nest near Webb Lake. Watch for wading birds, including tricolored and great blue herons, also sandhill cranes, foraging in the wet prairies. Common ground doves, logger-head shrikes, red-winged blackbirds, and eastern meadowlarks are common. Eastern diamondback rattlesnakes are plentiful. American woodcock and common snipe overwinter. Obtain a regulations summary and map at check station. Only the designated recreation area, about one-fifth of the total site, is open during the non-hunting season; during managed hunts in late fall, winter and spring, the entire acreage is open. Primitive camping only.

**Directions:** *South of Punta Gorda on Interstate 75, take exit 27 (Tucker's Grade). Travel east 0.25 mile to area entrance.*

DeLorme maps 104 and 105

**Ownership:** Florida Game and Fresh Water Fish Commission (941) 639-1531
**Size:** 65,770 acres
**Closest town:** Punta Gorda

*The northern bobwhite's call is a familiar sound in the pinewoods, where this small member of the quail family hunts along the ground for seeds and insects. The northern bobwhite is still a popular game bird throughout the state.*
MARESA PRYOR

**Description:** Seven miles of wide, white beach, acres of pine forest, oak/palm hammock, mangrove swamp and a spectacular display of bird life characterize this unspoiled barrier island at the mouth of Charlotte Harbor. Accessible only by private boat or ferry. Shelling and swimming are excellent.

**Viewing Information:** To observe a wide variety of shorebirds, walk south from the primitive cabins about one mile to Johnson Shoals, a large, C-shaped cove with productive mudflats close to Boca Grande Pass. August and September are the best months for shorebird observation—look for American oyster-catchers, black skimmers, long-billed curlews, plovers, whimbrels, gulls, and all of Florida's common tern species. Ospreys nest year-round on Cayo Costa, and brown pelicans are common residents as well. Magnificent frigatebirds soar overhead in summer months. On interior trails, look for sandy burrows of gopher tortoises. Primitive camping and rental cabins available.

*Directions: In North Fort Myers, take exit 26 from Interstate 75. Travel west on Florida Highway 78 for 20 miles to Pine Island. Turn right (north) on Stringfellow Road to Bokeelia; private ferry services take visitors to park. Call (941) 964-0375 for information. Ferries dock on island's bay side; walk one mile to beach or take park-operated tram.*

DeLorme maps 104-105

**Size:** 2,132 acres
**Ownership:** Department of Environmental Protection (941) 964-0375
**Closest town:** Boca Grande

*Ospreys are common residents of open freshwater and saltwater habitats in Florida. To distinguish the smaller osprey from a bald eagle (page 84), look for broad, dark cheek marks on the osprey's white head; dark brown back and white breast; and wings held crooked or angled in flight. Ospreys nest in standing dead trees, called snags, and plunge-dive from great heights to catch large fish.*
BARRY MANSELL

SOUTHWEST

**Description:** This recently-acquired wetland system acts as a natural travel corridor for wildlife by connecting northern Lee County to the Estero Bay area. Many animals, such as raccoons, gray squirrels, five-lined skinks, red-shouldered hawks, and wild turkey, are year-round residents. Other animals less frequently seen include bobcat, river otter, and white-tailed deer. Five distinct plant communities are clearly interpreted for the visitor on a 1.2-mile boardwalk trail. Hands-on mini-exhibits and an extremely informative pamphlet called the "Explorer's Companion" make the trip fun and interesting.

**Viewing Information:** Little blue herons, anhingas, American alligators, raccoons, red-shouldered hawks, and pileated woodpeckers are commonly seen all year. During the dry season (October-June), freshwater fish concentrate in depressions in the Slough called flag ponds. Here, great egrets, snowy egrets, tricolored herons, white ibis, and wood storks are easily visible as they feed and rest. Bald eagles may be spotted overhead from October-January, and migrating warblers and other songbirds can be plentiful in October and again in April. A photo blind, two observation platforms, and frequent seating areas further enhance the experience for wildlife viewers or photographers at Six Mile Cypress. Excellent barrier-free access.

**Directions:** *Exit Interstate 75 south of Fort Myers at Colonial Boulevard (Exit 22). Go west 0.5 mile to Six Mile Parkway. Turn left (south) and drive three miles. Turn left (east) on Penzance Boulevard to enter facility.*

DeLorme map 105

Ownership: Lee County (941) 432-2004
**Size:** 2,200 acres
**Closest town:** Fort Myers

*The fish-eating anhinga is nicknamed "snakebird" because of its snakelike appearance when swimming. Anhingas resemble cormorants but have a longer tail and neck and a slender, pointed bill. They often perch with wings extended to dry.*
JIM ROETZEL

**Description:** One of Florida's best wildlife observation sites. This heavily-visited refuge is located on the north side of subtropical Sanibel Island. High probability of seeing wildlife on walking and canoe trails, and the four-mile Wildlife Drive, an auto tour traversing brackish and freshwater impoundments. Drive is closed to all access on Fridays. Mottled duck, American swallow-tailed kite, roseate spoonbill, white ibis, wood stork, mangrove cuckoo, and gray kingbird are among the unique birds that inhabit this refuge.

**Viewing Information:** Nearly 300 bird species, more than 50 types of reptiles and amphibians, and at least 32 species of mammals use this refuge for shelter and sustenance. Sunrise, sunset, and low tide are best times to observe year-round wildlife residents, including osprey, brown pelican, roseate spoonbill, and many other wading bird species. American alligators bask along left side of Wildlife Drive on cool, sunny days. Warblers, vireos, and other songbirds migrate through the refuge March through May, and again in the fall. December through February, visitors can see blue-winged teal, red-breasted mergansers, white pelicans, and other winter visitors. Foot trails include the 0.3-mile Shell Mound Trail, two-mile Indigo Trail, and 1.75 miles of trails at the nearby Bailey Tract. Two marked canoe trails offer a different perspective on the refuge. Canoe rentals, interpretive tram, and naturalist-led tours available at Tarpon Bay. Excellent visitor center offers exhibits, audio-visual programs, and book sales.

**Directions:** *See map, opposite page*

DeLorme Map 110

**Ownership:** US Fish and Wildlife Service (941) 472-1100
**Size:** 6,354 acres
**Closest town:** Sanibel

*American white pelicans are spectacular winter visitors to Florida. They are easily identified by their white plumage and black-tipped wings. Unlike brown pelicans, these birds never dive for prey, but instead cooperatively "herd" fish into shallow waters, scooping them into their immense beaks.* JOE MAC HUDSPETH

SOUTHWEST

**Description:** This nature center, owned and managed by a nonprofit foundation, consists of 1,100 acres of interior ridges and wetlands on Sanibel Island. A considerable portion of the Sanibel River passes through the preserve, encouraging an unusual diversity of plant and animal life. Four miles of loop trails and an observation tower; excellent interpretive exhibits, guided tours, and a native plant nursery and store. A quieter, more subtle experience than nearby Ding Darling National Wildlife Refuge (site 96).

**Viewing Information:** Anole lizards rustle along every path and in the underbrush. In the marshy wetlands, observers may spot great and little blue herons, snowy and great egrets, white ibis, American coots, common moorhens, rails, and mottled ducks. Summering black-necked stilts are occasionally seen. Marsh rabbits feed along the edges of the grassy trails. Ospreys nest close to the observation tower and may often be seen overhead, along with black and turkey vultures and, in the summer, magnificent frigatebirds. On the drier sandy ridges, gopher tortoises dig their burrows and forage for succulent grasses and herbs. American alligators are spotted occasionally. Wintering robins and many other songbirds are abundant, including cardinals, woodpeckers, gray catbirds, rufous-sided towhees, wrens, and warblers.

*Directions:* See map

DeLorme map 110

**Ownership:** Sanibel-Captiva Conservation Foundation (941) 472-2329
**Size:** 1,100 acres
**Closest town:** Sanibel

*The green anole lizard is the only native anole found in Florida; the other four are West Indian species which have become established in the state. Green anoles are good climbers and display a striking pink throat fan.*
GAIL SHUMWAY

128

**Description:** This state park encompasses two special ecosystems of the southwest Florida coast: mangrove estuary and sandy barrier island, both in short supply throughout this heavily-developed region. Visitors walk or ride a tram through dense mangroves and over a tidal bay to the beach.

**Viewing Information:** Stroll across the 0.5-mile boardwalk to the beach. At low tide, watch for feeding snowy and great egrets, great blue, little blue, and tricolored herons, white ibis, double-crested cormorants, and, in spring and summer, roseate spoonbills. Also look among the arching prop roots of the red mangrove trees for clusters of coon oysters, and the raccoons that feed on them. Active fiddler crabs scavenge along the shoreline at low tide. Ospreys nest in dead trees near the water, and dive for fish in waters throughout the park. In summer, look for magnificent frigatebirds soaring aloft. On the beaches, brown pelicans and terns are frequently spotted, along with such shorebirds as the American oystercatcher. Reddish and snowy egrets often can be found foraging along the Gulf beach. Open every day 8:00 a.m. to sunset; closed Christmas Day. Parking fee. Entrance fee required.

**Directions:** *On Florida Highway 865 south of Fort Myers Beach, drive across the causeway over Big Carlos Pass into the park.*

DeLorme maps 110-111

**Ownership:** State of Florida (941) 463-4588
**Size:** 712 acres
**Closest town:** Bonita Beach

SOUTHWEST

*Don't confuse bright pink roseate spoonbills with non-native flamingos. Adult spoonbills have a white neck and orange tail. They swing their spatulate bills from side to side in shallow waters, capturing small fish, shrimp, snails, and fiddler crabs. Most spoonbills move south to the Everglades for the winter months (October-February).*
MICHAEL S. SAMPLE

**Description:** This site protects the headwaters of a vast wetland system that flows south into the Florida Panther National Wildlife Refuge and Corkscrew Swamp Sanctuary, through the Fakahatchee Strand, and eventually to Florida Bay. The property includes pine flatwoods, oak and palm hammocks, and the 5,000-acre Corkscrew Marsh.

**Viewing Information:** Three maintained hiking trails provide access to the major habitats. Some trails may be wet; check conditions at the entrance kiosk. Scan the skies for turkey vultures, swallow-tailed kites (spring and summer), and wood storks. Depending on water levels in the Corkscrew Marsh, egrets, herons, and alligators may be visible. You may get a glimpse of turkeys, deer, hogs, or gopher tortoises (and their burrows) along the flatwoods trails. Listen for barred owls in the hammock and the loud tapping of pileated woodpeckers in the pine flatwoods. Carnivorous plants such as sundews and yellow butterworts are common in moist areas. Panther and bear sign have been reported here; check the ground for tracks and scat. Only a few facilities are currently available at this site: an information kiosk, trail maps, and a portable toilet. An observation platform and other site enhancements are planned for the future.

**Directions:** *From Interstate 75, take exit 19 (Corkscrew Road). Go east on Corkscrew Road for 18 miles. The entrance is on the right. From Florida Highway 82 (Immokalee Road), take County Road 850 (Corkscrew Road) southwest for 1.5 miles. The entrance is on the left.*

DeLorme Map 111

**Ownership:** South Florida Water Management District and the Corkscrew Regional Ecosystem Watershed Land and Water Trust, Inc. (941) 332-7771
**Size:** 6,825 acres
**Closest Town:** Lehigh Acres

*Two species of vultures reside year-round in Florida and are often seen soaring high in the sky. The black vulture, shown here, has a black head and glides with its wings held in a flat profile. The turkey vulture has a red head and soars with its wings often held upward in a shallow V.*

JIM ROETZEL

**Description:** A unique two-mile boardwalk winds through pinelands, wet prairie, marsh, lakes, and the world's largest remaining subtropical old-growth bald cypress forest. In spring and summer months, enjoy splendid native ferns, orchids, bromeliads, and wildflowers.

**Viewing Information:** As the dry season approaches (January-April), wading birds, including little blue herons and white ibis, congregate with other wild-life in feeding pools close to the boardwalk trail. The largest nesting colony of wood storks in the United States raises its young during late winter, sometimes within full view of the boardwalk. Several hundred American swallow-tailed kites roost during summer months. Green-backed herons, anhingas, American egrets, great blue herons, and American bitterns are often sighted. Calling red-shouldered hawks and pileated woodpeckers are ever-present. During spring and fall migration, many species of warblers and other songbirds arrive. Alligators, turtles, river otters, barred owls, and limpkins can be viewed year-round. Painted buntings frequent the bird feeders near the visitor center in winter. Excellent opportunities for wildlife photographers. Specific wildlife sightings posted daily at the trailhead. Helpful self-guiding tour pamphlet available at visitor center. Open all year, December-April (7:00 a.m. to 5:00 p.m.); May-November (8:00 a.m. to 5:00 p.m.). *EXCELLENT BARRIER-FREE ACCESS.*

**Directions:** *From U.S. Highway 41 nine miles north of Naples, drive east 21 miles on Florida Highway 846. Turn left at sanctuary sign.*

DeLorme map 111

**Ownership:** National Audubon Society (941) 348-9151
**Size:** 10,560 acres
**Closest town:** Naples

🅿️ 💲 🚶 👥 🚏 ♿

*Nearly all United States nesting areas, or rookeries, for wood storks occur in Florida. But due to the drainage of wetlands, droughts, and human-altered water levels in the Everglades, wood storks are listed as endangered. In flight, these birds are easily identified by their out-stretched necks, seven-foot wingspan, and black tail and wing edges.*

BARRY MANSELL

SOUTHWEST

131

**Description:** Barefoot Beach is located on Little Hickory Island, a barrier island typical of those which line the Gulf and Atlantic coasts. The preserve is covered with mangrove forest, tropical hammock, and 8,200 feet of beach and low sand dunes. A one-mile-long, self-guided trail that interprets the coastal vegetation travels south to Wiggins Pass, along the interface between the sand dunes and tropical hammock.

**Viewing Information:** The nature trail begins from the overflow parking area at the south end of the park. Pick up a plant identification guide at the trailhead. Gopher tortoises and their burrows are plentiful along this trail, as are brown and green anoles. Mice, snakes, raccoons, opossums, bobcats, and foxes may also have left their marks in the sand. When the trail ends at the beach at Wiggins Pass, turn left and walk toward the mangrove forest. Wading birds may be feeding in this area. To return to the parking area, you may walk back along the nature trail or walk along the beach. If the latter route is chosen, scan the offshore waters for bottle-nosed dolphins. Look for willets, plovers, sandpipers, terns, and gulls on the shoreline. During the summer months, brown pelicans and ospreys are common. Look along the beach for sign of the Atlantic loggerhead sea turtles that nest here.

**Directions:** Take Bonita Beach Road (exit 18) from Interstate 75. Travel 5.6 miles on Bonita Beach Road to a left turn on Leley Boulevard (at park entrance sign). Follow the road 1.7 miles through residential development to the preserve.

DeLorme Map 111

**Ownership:** Collier County Department of Parks and Recreation (941) 591-4986
**Size:** 342 acres
**Closest town:** Bonita Springs

*When you take a break from birding and other wildlife watching in Florida, think about planting a mini-refuge for wild creatures in your own backyard. In southern Florida, and along the barrier islands through central Florida, the sea grape is a wonderful landscape choice. Its flowers are an important source of nectar for bees, and its fleshy fruit appeals not only to humans, but also to raccoons, turtles, and a host of native birds.* JEFF FOOTT

**Description:** This center serves as interpretive facility for the 9,200-acre Rookery Bay National Estuarine Research Reserve. A 0.5-mile self-guided boardwalk leads to an observation deck for viewing wading birds and other wildlife. Scrub oak, pine flatwood, mangrove forest, and marsh plant communities are traversed as elevation above sea level varies ever so slightly on this short walk. Two other short trails through mangrove forest and coastal hammock plant communities are also available within the reserve. From December through April, the center offers three different pontoon boat tours, focusing on birding, beachcombing, and mangrove ecology, in addition to canoe trips and other wilderness excursions. Call ahead for boat trip reservations.

**Viewing Information:** On the boardwalk, raccoons, gopher tortoises, belted kingfishers, several woodpecker species, and many songbirds are commonly seen and heard, especially early in the morning and in the late afternoon. At the observation deck, watch for ospreys and a variety of wading and shore birds, especially March-June, when the pond dries down and prey fish concentrate. On the trail and at the center's bird feeders, close encounters with Florida scrub-jays are likely. Admire native butterfly species in the newly-installed butterfly garden. On naturalist-led boat tours, ospreys and bald eagles, many wading bird species, double-crested cormorants, gulls, and brown pelicans are easily observed. Bottle-nosed dolphins and manatees (less frequent) may also be spotted.

**Directions:** *From U.S. Highway 41 (Tamiami Trail) south of Naples, turn right on Florida Highway 951, heading toward Marco Island. Travel 2.7 miles to Shell Island Road and turn right. Drive one mile to entrance on right.*

DeLorme map 111

**Ownership:** The Conservancy of Southwest Florida (941) 775-8569
**Size:** 13,000 acres
**Closest town:** Marco Island

A multitude of flowering plants in Florida, both native and exotic, nourish hundreds of butterfly species. Butterflies may feed on a great variety of nectar-producing plants, but each species has a specific host plant which the caterpillars (butterfly larvae) feed on almost exclusively. A pair of stunning zebra longwing butterflies are pictured here.
JOHN NETHERTON

SOUTHWEST

**Description:** One of Florida's great natural treasures. The long, forested swamp from which this preserve takes its name is the major drainage slough of Big Cypress Swamp. To the south, tidal swamps and great mangrove estuaries in the Ten Thousand Islands depend on Fakahatchee's infusion of fresh water. North America's largest stand of native royal palms grows here, along with abundant ferns and air plants. Orchids grow in the swamp's interior. Swamp lakes, marl prairies, hammocks, and cypress domes add diversity. Florida panther, Florida black bear, Everglades mink, and wood storks are among the threatened and endangered animals that survive here.

**Viewing Information:** Big Cypress Bend Boardwalk on U.S. Highway 41 is the easiest access to an old-growth cypress stand at the south end of the preserve. The quiet visitor may spot American alligators, basking turtles, and frolicking river otters. Look for wood storks, roseate spoonbills, white and glossy ibis, snowy and great egrets, tricolored, little blue and great blue herons, and night herons. To go deeper into the strand, a trip on Jane's Scenic Drive is a must. White-tailed deer, raccoons, and opossum are often visible at dawn and dusk, as well as the occasional bobcat and Florida black bear. Opportunities for day hikes are boundless on numbered logging tram roads. Number 12, East Main, is a good spot to brush up on wildlife track identification. Number 7 leads through junglelike swamp to Four Stakes Prairie. Tram trails may be seasonally wet. *VISITOR FACILITIES VERY LIMITED.* Maps available at ranger station on Jane's Scenic Drive.

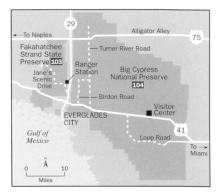

*Directions: See map*

DeLorme maps 112 and 116

**Ownership:** Department of Environmental Protection (941) 695-4593
**Size:** 65,000 acres
**Closest town:** Everglades City

*Cabbage palm islands, known as "hammocks," rise above grassy prairies in parts of the Fakahatchee Strand. This natural area sends vital fresh water to the Ten Thousand Islands, a great mangrove wilderness to the south.*

HELEN LONGEST-SLAUGHTER

134

**Description:** On this preserve, "big" refers to the vast landscape, not the size of the trees. At one time, Big Cypress contained pristine cypress strands and old-growth pinelands, but by 1950 virtually all the ancient trees had been logged. The young cypress strands, mixed-hardwood swamps, and pinelands in the preserve today are still recovering. Big Cypress is noted for its wide-spread prairies dotted with dwarf cypress trees. Throughout the wet season, the preserve is flooded and serves as a natural reservoir and nutrient filter, much as the Everglades do. Essential habitat is provided here for bald eagles, a large concentration of red-cockaded woodpeckers, and the imperiled Florida panther. The primary visitors to Big Cypress are hunters and off-road vehicle users. At present, access and interpretation for the general public is limited.

**Viewing Information:** During the dry winter months, an abundance of wildlife is concentrated along deep pools and sloughs. Borrow canals along Turner River Road and Birdon Road (both gravel) are good places to spot alligators and many wading birds, including wood storks, white and glossy ibis, great blue, little blue, and tricolored herons, as well as night herons, great and snowy egrets, and anhingas. The Loop Road south from Monroe Station also provides good viewing, but the road is in extremely poor condition. Stop at the Big Cypress National Preserve Visitor Center on U.S.Highway 41 for visitor information and restrooms.

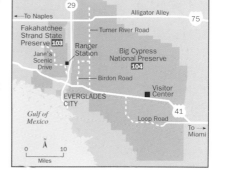

**Directions:** *See map*

DeLorme maps 112, 113, 116 and 117

**Ownership:** National Park Service (941) 695-4111
**Size:** 729,000
**Closest town:** Everglades City

*The tawny Florida panther is a subspecies of cougar that has adapted to the subtropical environment of Florida. Less than 50 panthers still remain in Florida, making this animal one of the rarest and most endangered mammals in the world. Panthers are very secretive and avoid humans.*
GAIL SHUMWAY

SOUTHWEST

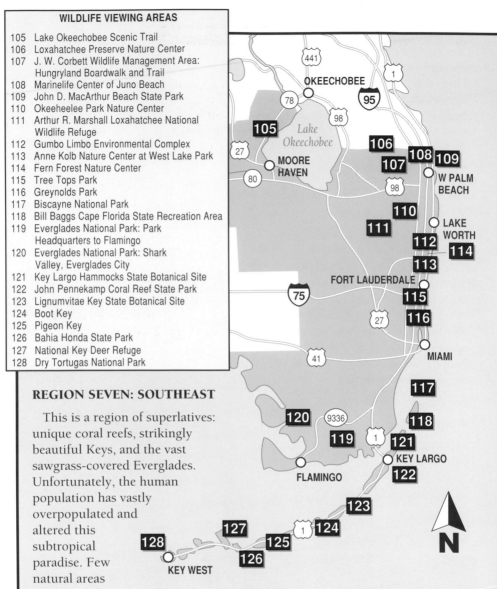

## WILDLIFE VIEWING AREAS

105 Lake Okeechobee Scenic Trail
106 Loxahatchee Preserve Nature Center
107 J. W. Corbett Wildlife Management Area: Hungryland Boardwalk and Trail
108 Marinelife Center of Juno Beach
109 John D. MacArthur Beach State Park
110 Okeeheelee Park Nature Center
111 Arthur R. Marshall Loxahatchee National Wildlife Refuge
112 Gumbo Limbo Environmental Complex
113 Anne Kolb Nature Center at West Lake Park
114 Fern Forest Nature Center
115 Tree Tops Park
116 Greynolds Park
117 Biscayne National Park
118 Bill Baggs Cape Florida State Recreation Area
119 Everglades National Park: Park Headquarters to Flamingo
120 Everglades National Park: Shark Valley, Everglades City
121 Key Largo Hammocks State Botanical Site
122 John Pennekamp Coral Reef State Park
123 Lignumvitae Key State Botanical Site
124 Boot Key
125 Pigeon Key
126 Bahia Honda State Park
127 National Key Deer Refuge
128 Dry Tortugas National Park

## REGION SEVEN: SOUTHEAST

This is a region of superlatives: unique coral reefs, strikingly beautiful Keys, and the vast sawgrass-covered Everglades. Unfortunately, the human population has vastly overpopulated and altered this subtropical paradise. Few natural areas remain on the coast, although sea turtles still nest on protected beaches.

West of Lake Okeechobee, Florida's largest lake, swallow-tailed kites congregate mid-summer before migrating south. The Everglades, world-famous river of grass, stretches many miles wide, but only inches deep. Wading birds, including wood storks, roseate spoonbills, great egrets, great blue herons, snowy egrets, and white and glossy ibis nest here, although in ever-declining numbers. American alligators are abundant, and the only population of endangered crocodiles in Florida is found in the Keys.

Tropical hardwood hammocks are home to tiny Key deer, tree snails, and rare butterflies. Unique birds live in these and other Keys habitats, including the white-crowned pigeon, gray kingbird, and mangrove cuckoo. Reddish egrets, roseate spoonbills, and other wading birds nest on remote keys, and forage in shallow Florida Bay.

**Description:** *AUTO TOUR.* Florida's largest lake receives the flow of the Kissimmee River from the northwest and drains south into the Everglades. Encircling the lake is a large dike intended to reduce flood damage. The lake has been abused by dairy and stormwater run-off, and invaded by exotic weeds, but still harbors impressive concentrations of wildlife. Fall and winter are the best times for this forty-mile auto tour of the lake's northwestern rim.

**Viewing Information and Directions:** Two miles south of Okeechobee at the intersection of U.S. Highway 441 and Florida 78, stop at the Parrot Avenue Wayside Park. Take the boardwalk over the marshy edge of the lake and look for herons, egrets, and wintering waterfowl, especially ring-necked ducks. Continue southwest on Florida 78, watching for snail kites. The Okee-tante Recreation Area (see map below), five miles south, along with the Indian Prairie and Harney Pond canal access areas, are good spots to pause and look for wood storks, white ibis, anhingas, limpkins, great blue and little blue herons, and snowy and great egrets. Wintering American coots are abundant. On the right, dry prairies interspersed with oak-cabbage palm hammocks—called palm savannas—are primary habitat for crested caracara, burrowing owls, and sandhill cranes. In winter, huge numbers of turkey and black vultures gather and ride the updrafts along the levees. Farther south, near Fisheating Creek Wayside Park, as many as 600 swallow-tailed kites converge June through August, preparing to migrate south for the winter. Late afternoons and early mornings are the best times to observe them. American alligators, turtles, frogs, and water snakes are common in Okeechobee marshes.

DeLorme maps 101 and 107

**Ownership:** State of Florida; Florida 78 canal access areas managed by Florida Department of Transportation
**Closest towns:** Okeechobee, Moore Haven

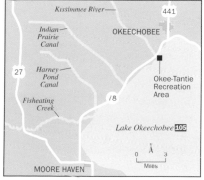

Dry and wet prairies in central and south Florida are among the most important, but unprotected, wildlife areas in the state. Crested caracaras, southern bald eagles, burrowing owls, sandhill cranes, scrub jays, snail kites, mottled ducks, red-cockaded woodpeckers, and other rare species contribute to the region's rich biodiversity.

**SOUTHEAST**

**Description:** The nature center sits at the north end of the city of West Palm Beach Water Catchment Area (WCA), a 19-square mile wetland of cypress and wet prairies. The WCA supplies drinking water for the surrounding communities and helps to protect the Loxahatchee Slough, headwaters of the Loxahatchee River.

**Viewing Information:** This new site offers panoramic views of a pristine shallow sawgrass prairie and cypress swamp from the nature center and the 1,500-foot-long boardwalk. Common wading birds include great blue herons, great egrets, ibises, and limpkins. Look for black-necked stilts in the summer. Turkey vultures and red-shouldered hawks are regular year-round sights. Watch for alligators, turtles, and, rarely, otters. Occasionally, snail kites and bald eagles are spotted. On the north side of Northlake Boulevard, the Eagle and Hammock trails, each 0.5 mile long, traverse upland habitats. Look for evidence of raccoon, armadillo, and wild hog. At a freshwater marsh overlook on the Eagle Trail, watch for wading birds. This site is rapidly expanding its facilities and hours of operation. It is best to call ahead for current conditions. Guided canoe outings and evening presentations are regularly offered.

*Directions: From West Palm Beach, take Interstate 95 north to the Northlake Boulevard exit. Head west on Northlake Boulevard for approximately four miles. The entrance to the center is on the left on Northlake Boulevard, one mile west of the intersection of Northlake Boulevard and the Beeline Highway (Florida Highway 710).*

DeLorme Map 109

**Ownership:** City of West Palm Beach (561) 627-8831

**Size:** 12,160 acres

**Closest town:** Palm Beach Gardens

*Nine-banded armadillos, native to South and Central America, arrived in Florida earlier this century as circus escapees and via natural range expansion from Mexico and Texas. The armored bands protect this slow moving mammal from predators as it waddles along, digging shallow holes in search of insects.*

JEFF FOOTT

## 107 J.W. CORBETT WILDLIFE MANAGEMENT AREA: HUNGRYLAND BOARDWALK AND TRAIL

**Description:** There is a special solitude to be discovered here, along with the chance to appreciate several increasingly rare native plant communities. A 1.2-mile trail and boardwalk pass through southern slash pine flatwoods, a sawgrass marsh, an oak/cabbage palm hammock, and a cypress wetland lush with bromeliads and ferns. This site is fairly new, and adjacent to 60,244-acre J. W. Corbett Wildlife Management Area. A spur of the Florida Trail can be accessed from this site. Frequent prescribed fires improve visibility and habitat conditions for numerous wildlife species.

**Viewing Information:** Look for white-tailed deer and bobcats in early morning and late afternoon. Pileated woodpeckers, and barred and screech owls forage in the cypress dome. River otters and raccoons are sometimes seen near the boardwalk. Look for herons, egrets, and common yellowthroats in the marshes. The red-shouldered hawk is commonly heard. Check the oak hammock and cypresses for large numbers of migratory warblers in the spring and fall. Good interpretive signs describe the plant and animal communities. Although there are seasonal hunts in the surrounding wildlife management area, there is a no-hunting safety zone around the site.

**Directions:** *From West Palm Beach, take Interstate 95 north to Northlake Boulevard exit. Go west approximately 12.3 miles, crossing the Beeline Expressway (Florida Highway 710). Turn right on Seminole Pratt Whitney Road. The entrance to the J. W. Corbett Wildlife Management Area is visible to the left. Follow signs to the Hungryland Boardwalk and Trail, 0.7 mile from the check station to grassy parking area.*

DeLorme map 109

**Ownership:** Florida Game and Fresh Water Fish Commission (561) 625-5122
**Size:** 1.2-mile trail
**Closest town:** Palm Beach Gardens

*The Hungryland boardwalk and trail offers exploration of usually inaccessible cypress swamp. Here the trees grow in characteristic "strands" along seasonal streams, or in rounded "domes."*

HELEN LONGEST-SLAUGHTER

SOUTHEAST

139

**Description:** There is a wealth of information to be found at this tiny non-profit educational facility in Loggerhead Park, across from the Atlantic Ocean. Saltwater tanks and exhibits introduce visitors to the loggerhead, leatherback, and green sea turtles which nest along Florida's Atlantic beaches. A wide variety of other common marine animals are featured as well. Public turtle walks are scheduled during the nesting season in June and July; *RESERVATIONS REQUIRED*. A winter lecture series on various marine conservation topics runs from December through April. Loggerhead Park has parking, restroom, and picnic facilities for visitors to the public beach.

**Viewing Information:** The visitor center, staffed almost entirely by volunteers, is open year-round Tuesday through Saturday from 10:00 a.m. to 3:00 p.m., Sundays noon to 3:00 p.m. Beach and park are open all year from dawn to 11:00 p.m. A lookout tower within a two-acre section of coastal scrub near the Marinelife Center provides a nice view of the ocean. Look for sea turtle tracks along the beach in early morning. Watch for brown pelicans, laughing and ring-billed gulls flying along the beach, and willets, sanderlings, and dunlins feeding along the shoreline.

*Directions: From Interstate 95 in Palm Beach Gardens, take exit 57 onto Florida Highway 786 (PGA Boulevard). Travel east approximately three miles to U.S. Highway 1. Go north on U.S. Highway 1 for three miles. Entrance to the park is on the right, just after the intersection of U.S. 1 and Donald Ross Road.*

DeLorme map 109

**Ownership:** Private facility within county park (561) 627-8280
**Closest town:** Juno Beach

*Green turtles were once abundant in the marine waters of south Florida. Today 60-800 females nest along the eastern coastline of the state each year, mostly between Volusia and Broward counties. The broad expanses of shallow, sandy flats covered with seagrasses are preferred green turtle feeding grounds.*

FRED WHITEHEAD

**Description:** Pristine Atlantic beaches, vegetated dunes, mangrove estuary, and subtropical coastal hammock on a barrier island offer a haven from surrounding development.

**Viewing Information:** Self-guided nature trails identify the temperate and subtropical trees found in the coastal hammock. A 1,600-foot boardwalk crosses Lake Worth Cove and ends at the beach. A short trail with several dune crossovers runs south behind the dunes. The shallow waters of the estuary attract roseate spoonbills in the summer, and ospreys, herons, brown pelicans, anhingas, and snowy egrets throughout the year. Fiddler crabs scuttle among the roots of the mangroves. Large numbers of loggerhead, green, and leatherback turtles nest along the beach in the summer. Inquire about ranger-led walks to search for nesting loggerheads in June and July. Scan the beach for gulls, terns, and shorebirds. Look and listen for red-bellied and pileated woodpeckers around the excellent nature center, open 9:00 a.m. to 5:00 p.m. Wednesday through Monday (closed Tuesday). A good video program is available upon request and special programs on a broad range of natural history topics are offered throughout the year. When exiting the park, continue south on Florida Highway A1A to where the road crosses Lake Worth over the small Burnt Bridge. Wading birds are sometimes concentrated here at low tide.

**Directions:** *From U.S. Highway 1 in North Palm Beach, turn east onto Ocean Boulevard (Florida Highway A1A South) and drive 1.8 miles to park entrance.*

DeLorme map 109

**Ownership:** Department of Environmental Protection (561) 624-6950
**Size:** 225 acres
**Closest town:** North Palm Beach

*Flocks of laughing gulls and ring-billed gulls are a common year-round sight in Florida. Laughing gulls are primarily coastal birds feeding on fish and other marine organisms. In the summer, the adult bird's mottled gray head changes to black, making for easy identification. The ring-billed gull is frequently seen on the coast, as well as in huge flocks in shopping center parking lots and sanitary landfills.*

JOHN NETHERTON

SOUTHEAST

141

**Description:** The 100-acre Okeeheelee Nature Center is located in one corner of a 1,000-acre regional recreational park. Except for this small area, the entire park was created out of land intensively mined for shell rock in the 1960s. The primary focus of the nature center is restoration—encouraging the native flora and fauna associated with the native pine uplands and removing exotic plants.

**Viewing Information:** Visit the nature center to obtain a detailed trail guide. The trails are open every day, sunrise to sunset. The nature center buildings and exhibits are closed on Mondays all year, and on Sundays from Memorial Day weekend to Labor Day weekend. The nature center offers approximately one mile of paved trail and almost 1.5 miles of shell rock trail. Look for gopher tortoises and their burrows along the pine trail. In winter, the East Marsh Trail is a good place to look for coots, common moorhens, ring-necked ducks, blue-winged and green-winged teals, pied-billed grebes, and wood ducks. Watch for red-tailed hawks and ospreys overhead. For nature center program information, call (561) 233-1400.

**Directions:** *From Interstate 95, take the Forest Hill Boulevard exit and travel west on Forest Hill Boulevard for about five miles. The entrance to the park is on the right, about one mile west of Jog Road. Once in the park, follow the signs for more than one mile to the nature center. The Florida Turnpike forms the western boundary of the park, but there is no access to Forest Hill Boulevard.*

DeLorme Map 109

**Ownership:** Palm Beach County Parks and Recreation Department (561) 966-6636
**Size:** 100 acres
**Closest town:** Greenacres

*The atala butterfly is a rare and endangered Florida species, limited to Key Biscayne. The larvae of this species feed only on native coontie plants and imported cycad plants used in landscaping.*
MICHAEL P. TURCO

The black bill and golden feet of the snowy egret distinguish it from all other wading birds. Note the beautiful, lacy breeding plumage; these feathers, raised and fanned during mating displays, were coveted by plume hunters earlier this century. Snowy egrets are no longer hunted, but habitat loss has caused their numbers to decrease.
GAIL SHUMWAY

**Description:** The Loxahatchee Refuge preserves part of the vast wetland wilderness known as the northern Everglades. Dikes along the edge of the refuge separate marsh and swampland from rapidly encroaching agricultural and residential development. Wading birds, shorebirds, and wintering waterfowl often concentrate here; birding can be excellent.

**Viewing Information:** Start at the visitor center (open weekdays 9:00 a.m. to 4:00 p.m., weekends and holidays 9:00 a.m. to 4:30 p.m.) for a good introduction to the refuge. The 0.4-mile Cypress Swamp Boardwalk is a lush area of cypress trees, ferns, and air plants. Listen for woodpeckers and look for basking snakes and anoles. The 0.8-mile Marsh Trail encircles a freshwater impoundment and has an observation tower. Herons, egrets, ibis, limpkins, American coots, anhingas, vultures, ospreys, and red-shouldered hawks are common year-round; many nest on the refuge. In winter, look for blue-winged teal, ring-necked ducks, wood ducks, and fulvous whistling ducks. American alligators are common. Longer dike trails and canoe trails invite exploration.

*Directions: From Interstate 95 (exit 44) in Boynton Beach, travel seven miles west to U.S. Highway 441; turn south. Drive two miles to refuge entrance on west side of road.*

DeLorme map 108,109,114,115

**Ownership:** U.S. Fish and Wildlife Service (561) 734-8303
**Size:** 145,635 acres
**Closest town:** Boynton Beach

*The fulvous whistling duck is primarily a nocturnal feeder on the seeds of grasses and weeds in open marshlands, wet prairies, or flooded agricultural fields. The dark wings and rich buff-yellow plumage on the head, neck, and underparts distinguish this handsome bird.* WILLIAM J. WEBER

**Description:** Florida's tropical hardwood hammock and mangrove communities, once so prevalent along the southeastern coast, are well-represented at this costal island preserve. Its location west of Red Reef Park, between the Intracoastal Waterway and the Atlantic Ocean, allows for the study of both the marine and estuarine habitats. There is a boardwalk through the mangrove and hammock communities and a forty-foot-high observation tower. Large saltwater tanks, smaller aquariums, and other exhibits acquaint the visitor with the tropical plants and animals.

**Viewing Information:** This complex was designed to provide environmental education to the community. Classes, seminars, workshops, and field trips are regularly offered. Call ahead for schedules. The facility is open from 9:00 a.m. to 4:00 p.m. Monday through Saturday, and noon to 4:00 p.m. on Sunday. Acreage is small and is surrounded by a densely populated area, so much of the wildlife observed is captive. Exhibits include snakes, baby sea turtles, and saltwater fish. Brown pelicans, ospreys, ring billed and laughing gulls, raccoons and gray squirrels, and land crabs may be observed year-round. The facility is partially barrier-free.

**Directions:** *In Boca Raton, take Interstate 95 to Palmetto Park Road (exit 39). Drive east on Palmetto Park Road for four miles until it ends at Florida Highway A1A. Turn left. Continue 1.2 miles to entrance on left.*

DeLorme map 115

**Ownership:** City of Boca Raton (561) 338-1473
**Size:** 20 acres
**Closest town:** Boca Raton

*Where there is ocean, there are crabs, and Florida boasts a wide variety of these hardy animals, from large groups of fiddler crabs scuttling among saltmarsh grasses to the ghost crabs scurrying to their burrows in drier parts of the beaches.*
DOUG PERRINE

SOUTHEAST

**Description:** Within Broward County's high-density urban area, this park preserves 1,500 acres of mangrove wetlands, the largest such habitat in the 85-mile stretch from Biscayne Bay to West Palm Beach.

**Viewing Information:** Inquire at the exhibit hall about the 40-minute environmental boat tour of West Lake, a man-made lake dredged out in the 1920s. Canoes, kayaks, and jon boats are available for rent here; four canoe trails flow through the park. From the visitor center, walk the Mud Flat Trail to see fiddler and mangrove crabs. White ibis, Wilson's plover, and spotted sandpiper probe in the mud on exposed flats. From the overlooks along the Lake Observation Trail, look for great blue herons, yellow-crowned night herons, and the occasional roseate spoonbill feeding in shallow water. Ospreys are commonly seen in flight or sitting on exposed perches in West Lake. Park open 8:00 a.m. to 6:00, 6:30, or 7:30 p.m., depending on time of year. Exhibit Hall, featuring a stocked 3,500 gallon aquarium, is open 9:00 a.m. to 5:00 p.m.

**Directions:** *From Interstate 95, take exit 24, turn east onto Sheridan Street, and travel approximately 2.5 miles. The entrance to West Lake Park Recreation Area (and canoe marina) is on the right. To access the nature center complex, tour boat dock, and fishing pier, continue east on Sheridan Street and look for the entrance on the left, just before the Intracoastal Waterway bridge.*

DeLorme Map 115

**Ownership:** Broward County
Parks and Recreation Division
(954) 926-2410
**Size:** 1,500 acres
**Closest town:** Hollywood

*The yellow-crowned night heron is a stout, thick-billed heron with a gray body, black head, and white crown and cheek patch. Like the black-crowned night heron, it has a hunched posture when perched or standing.*

TOM VEZO

**Description:** This 254-acre island of greenery in heavily-populated Broward County shelters songbirds, small mammals, reptiles, amphibians, and butterflies. Purchased as a Designated Urban Wilderness Site in 1978, the site preserves a lovely remnant of south Florida's natural heritage.

**Viewing Information:** On the Prairie Overlook Trail, meandering through open prairie and oak/cabbage palm communities, visitors may spot a red-shouldered hawk, many songbirds, and gray squirrels. Early in the morning, quiet visitors should look for raccoon or opossum. Gray fox and bobcat are infrequently seen. During the winter (dry) season, the Cypress Creek Trail, a 0.5-mile barrier-free boardwalk, is a good place to look for tracks of mammals, along with such wading birds as the green-backed heron. In the tropical hardwood hammock and the cypress-maple swamp, many of the park's 32 species of ferns occur along with several species of bromeliads. Don't miss the arboretum, a labeled, living exhibit of native shrubs and trees especially favored by the park's butterflies. Black and yellow striped zebra and orange ruddy daggerwings are common. Interpretive center. A new sensory awareness trail was opened in 1995.

***Directions:*** *From Interstate 95, take exit 34 to Atlantic Boulevard in Pompano Beach. Travel west 2.9 miles to Lyons Road South and turn left (south). Park entrance on right.*

DeLorme map 115

**Ownership:** Broward County (954) 970-0150
**Size:** 254 acres
**Closest town:** Pompano Beach

Wildlife viewing takes a little practice and a good deal of patience. Move slowly and quietly. Stop frequently, scanning the terrain in every direction. Listen for rustling noises, bird songs, and splashing water. Stand or sit in a hidden place if at all possible. An observation blind, however crude, is ideal.

SOUTHEAST

**Description:** This urban park features nature and equestrian trails winding through dense woodland, including a magnificent oak hammock. The best wildlife viewing area within the park is a newly-restored freshwater marsh near the park's entrance. Many ducks and wading birds are concentrated here. A 1,000-foot boardwalk with viewing platforms offers excellent opportunities to observe abundant bird life.

**Viewing Information:** From the Tree Tops Center parking lot, follow the marsh boardwalk trail to the eastern side of the wetland. In open water areas in winter, look for mottled ducks, blue-winged and green-winged teal, American coots, and belted kingfishers. Common moorhens and pied-billed grebes nest in the marshes. Great egrets, anhingas, ospreys, red-winged blackbirds, and great blue, little blue and green-backed herons are predictable year-round. Butterflies are abundant. Bird walks are offered; call for details.

*Directions: See map*

DeLorme map 115

**Ownership:** Broward County (954) 370-3750
**Size:** 358 acres
**Closest town:** Davie

*(map showing:* To I-75, SW 100th Avenue, Knob Hill Road, Golden Shoe Road, Tree Tops Park 115, SW 45th Street, Orange Drive, To I-75, Griffin Road, University Drive, 817, 595, DAVIE, Florida's Turnpike, 818, Turnpike Exit 53, 0–1 Miles*)*

Some natural communities in Florida now remain only as small fragments, or habitat islands, requiring intensive management if they are to survive. Controlled burning, water level manipulation, and removal of invasive, non-native plants and animals are some of the strategies used by land managers to maximize the usefulness of these habitat patches to wildlife.

**Description:** The highlight of this pleasant urban park is a wading bird rookery located between a golf course and residential housing in northern Dade County. Trails encircle a mangrove wetland and afford close-up views of courtship activities, nest building, and the rearing of young.

**Viewing Information:** Nesting activity begins in earnest in late February, continues through the summer months, and declines in October. Expect to see great egrets, anhingas, double-crested cormorants, cattle egrets, white ibis, and green-backed, little blue, and tricolored herons. These birds also roost year-round in the park; the greatest concentrations are in the evening when the birds return for the night. Guided bird walks run throughout the year. Call ahead for reservations (305) 662-4124.

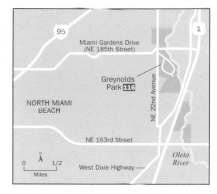

**Directions:** See map

DeLorme map 119

**Ownership:** Dade County
(305) 945-3425
**Size:** 230 acres
**Closest town:** North Miami Beach

*Herons, egrets, and brown pelicans are a few of the many birds that nest in colonies, or rookeries, congregating in groups that may number into the thousands. Rookeries are believed to offer nesting birds greater protection against predators, and, especially for young birds, increased feeding success, as they can follow older birds to good feeding areas. Rookeries should be observed from a distance to minimize disturbance during critical nesting periods.* JEFF FOOTT

SOUTHEAST

**Description:** A marine park that features exploration of the coral reefs and undeveloped keys of Biscayne Bay, southeast of Miami. Ninety-five percent of the park is underwater. Glass-bottom boat tours, snorkeling, and camping take place on the keys, accessible only by boat. No camping on the mainland.

**Viewing Information:** The three-hour glass-bottom boat tour is an excellent introduction to the dazzling corals and fishes in the reef community. Park headquarters, visitor center, and boat concession are located at Convoy Point, nine miles east of Homestead. Canoe rental and snorkel/scuba trips are also available. Most of the keys are small and densely covered with mangroves and tropical hardwoods, but several of the larger ones have boat docks, campgrounds, and nature trails. Park videos at visitor center. Double-crested cormorants, royal terns, black skimmers, and shorebirds are sometimes clustered on the stone jetty near the visitor center. As the boat passes the small, undeveloped keys, scan the mangroves for ospreys, double-crested cormorants, and brown pelicans. *A CORAL REEF IS ALIVE AND EXTREMELY FRAGILE. IT IS ILLEGAL TO COLLECT CORALS OR TROPICAL FISH.* If using a private boat, check with a ranger for buoy locations and boating regulations.

*Directions: In Homestead, take Exit 2 off Florida Turnpike (Homestead extension) onto Campbell Drive. Follow signs to North Canal Drive (SW 328th Street), continue to end of road. Or, from U.S. Highway 1 in Homestead, turn east onto North Canal Drive, continue to end of road.*

DeLorme map 122 and 123

**Ownership:** National Park Service (305) 230-1144
**Size:** 181,500 acres
**Closest town:** Homestead

*The red mangrove is one of four species of mangroves anchoring sheltered tidal flats in south Florida. It is the pioneer plant in these habitats and is easily identified by its prop roots, which arch into the water and provide shelter for oysters, crabs, mollusks, fish, and other marine animals.*

JEFF RIPPLE

**Description:** Cape Florida is located on the tip of Key Biscayne, a barrier island close to downtown Miami. In an impressive replanting effort, five native plant communities are being restored after extensive damage by Hurricane Andrew in 1992. Pedestrian and bicycle trails loop through the park.

**Viewing Information:** Prior to Hurricane Andrew's destruction, this park was an excellent birding site during migrations. As the newly planted native vegetation matures, the park is attracting greater numbers of land birds, and once again offers productive birding. The fall is a good time to see migratory raptors, including less-common species such as peregrine falcon and merlin Walk the 1.2-mile sandy beach and the southern edge of the restored 54-acre saltwater wetlands to look for laughing gulls, royal and caspian terns, ruddy turnstones, sanderlings, and other shorebirds. Check the five new freshwater wetlands for egrets and other wading birds. Walk, bicycle, or skate on the paved loop trail and watch for raccoons and marsh rabbits. Hummingbirds and butterflies are attracted to flowers in the interior coastal strand habitat. In the winter, manatees and dolphins can occasionally be seen in the harbor and along the western seawall. This popular park can host large crowds, so early morning visits provide the best opportunity for quiet wildlife viewing. A concession offers a variety of rentals, including bicycles and kayaks. Overnight boat camping is available for a fee in No Name Harbor.

**Directions:** *From Miami, take U.S. Highway 1 or Interstate 95 to the Rickenbacker Causeway and follow signs to Key Biscayne. Once on Key Biscayne, follow Crandon Boulevard south through the town of Key Biscayne to the park entrance.*

DeLorme Map 119

**Ownership:** Florida Department of Environmental Protection (305) 361-8779
**Size:** 406 acres
**Closest town:** Key Biscayne

*Helmetlike horseshoe crabs (not really crabs at all) are common along Florida's beaches in the spring, when they come ashore to mate and lay eggs. Their sharp, pointed tail is not used for defense, but as a rudder and as a burrowing aid.*

JIM ROETZEL

SOUTHEAST

151

**Description:** One of the world's extraordinary natural areas, the Everglades occupy over a million acres at the southern tip of Florida. Diverse habitats range from marine, estuarine, and mangrove communities to pinelands, hardwood hammocks, and extensive freshwater sloughs and prairies. Restoration projects are attempting to reverse damage wrought by agriculture and development. Main park entrances include Shark Valley, Royal Palm, or Everglades City. The best time to visit is November through April.

**Viewing Information:** The drive from park headquarters to Flamingo, a stretch of 38 miles, traverses several habitats and offers numerous interpretive facilities, boardwalks, and hiking and canoe trails along the route. The 0.5-mile Anhinga Trail over Taylor Slough provides excellent viewing of anhingas, herons, egrets, American alligators, turtles, and fishes. Nearby, a walk through a tropical hammock along the Gumbo Limbo Trail will demonstrate the remarkable recovery of this plant community from the ravages of Hurricane Andrew. Near the Flamingo campground, Eco Pond can be a good place to watch herons and white ibis. Boat tours, canoe and bike rentals available.

***Directions:*** *Take Florida's Turnpike south to its terminus in Florida City. Turn right on S.W. 344 Street (Palm Drive) and follow the signs on Florida Highway 9336 to Everglades National Park.*

DeLorme maps 121 and 122

**Ownership:** National Park Service (305) 242-7700
**Closest Town:** Florida City

*Egrets, ibises, herons, and roseate spoonbills sometimes congregate in large numbers in small ponds during the winter months, when water levels are low elsewhere in Everglades National Park. Bring binoculars and cameras and set up bright and early—most activity occurs around sunrise.* LARRY LIPSKY

**Description and Viewing Information: Shark Valley.** Located at the northern boundary of the park, this area features the sawgrass prairies of Shark River Slough. Tropical hardwood hammocks and tree islands dot the open landscape. Walk, bicycle (rentals available), or take a two-hour tram ride to an observation tower in the heart of the slough. Numerous fish, wading birds, and American alligators may be seen in and around borrow ponds below the tower. Watch for white-tailed deer at the edges of tree islands. Red-shouldered hawks, snail kites, northern harriers, and occasional rare short-tailed kites hunt the open prairies. Watch for bitterns and purple gallinules in the marsh. Reservations recommended for tram tour, December through March; call (305) 221-8455. Entry fee, restrooms, parking, and barrier-free access. **Everglades City.** The watery wilderness of Ten Thousand Islands, accessible only by boat or canoe, comprises the park's western edge. Manatees, bottle-nosed dolphins, American alligators, rays, sharks, nesting ospreys, and many wading birds, including roseate spoonbills and white ibis, may be spotted in this exceptionally beautiful setting. At the visitor center, obtain either maps and a backcountry permit for boat or canoe, or sign up for concession boat tours. Call for daily schedule and reservations, (941) 695-2591. Parking, restrooms, and boat ramp available.

*Directions: Shark Valley: From Interstate 95 in Miami, travel west on U.S. Highway 41 for 35 miles. Park entrance is on south side of road. Everglades City: Travel south 4.8 miles on Florida Highway 29 from the intersection with Tamiami Trail.*

**Ownership:** National Park Service (305) 242-7700
**Closest town:** Miami (Shark Valley); Everglades City
DeLorme maps 116-118 and 121-122

SOUTHEAST

*Alligators are normally afraid of people, but will lose their fear and approach if they are fed. Once an alligator loses its innate fear, it can become aggressive and extremely dangerous. Thousands are killed each year for this reason.* MICHAEL S. SAMPLE

**Description:** This site protects the largest remaining West Indian hardwood hammock in the continental United States. The rockland hammocks of northern Key Largo, which grow on limestone formed by a coral reef, hold a diverse collection of plants and invertebrates, most of tropical origin. Nearly 100 tree species are found in the park. A 1.75-mile nature trail and self-guiding trail brochures are available at the park entrance. At the north end of the park, nearly four miles of paved roads have been closed to motor vehicles, but remain available for hiking and biking. The park is open daily, 8 a.m. to sunset.

**Viewing Information:** Breeding mangrove cuckoos and black-whiskered vireos are often seen and heard during May and June. White-crowned pigeons can be seen in the park year-round. From December through April, white pelicans, grebes, moorhens, roseate spoonbills, wood storks, and other wading birds often aggregate in ponds near the north end of the park. Rare tree snails and giant land crabs are active, being most visible from May through November. Mosquitoes, biting flies, and gnats are sometimes abundant during those same months. You may spot raccoons, opossums, or grey squirrels on the trails at any time. Rarely seen species also found in the park include American crocodile, Key Largo woodrat and cotton mouse, short-tailed hawk, eastern diamondback rattlesnake, and eastern indigo snake.

**Directions:** *County Road 905 leaves the Overseas Highway (U.S. Highway 1) near mile marker 106.5, and runs along the western boundary of the park for nearly 11 miles. The park entrance, framed by a large masonry archway, is on the east (right) side of the road, less than a mile north of U.S. Highway 1.*

**Ownership:** Florida Department of Environmental Protection (305) 451-1202
**Size:** 2,500 acres
**Closest town:** Key Largo

*The American crocodile is much less common than Florida's other large reptile, the American alligator. It lives only in the brackish and saltwaters off the southern tip of Florida and in the Florida Keys. The crocodile's snout is narrow and tapering; the alligator's is broad.* JEFF FOOTT

**Description:** Established to protect a segment of the only living coral reef in the continental U.S., this park is renowned for its spectacular reefs and associated marine life. Glass-bottom boat tours make the five-mile trip out to the reefs three times daily. On the upland acreage there is a tropical hammock nature trail and a boardwalk through a mangrove swamp. This park receives very high visitation and temporarily closes its gates as necessary. Swimming, snorkeling, boating, and camping are the most popular activities.

**Viewing Information:** Start at the visitor center (open 8:00 a.m. to 5:00 p.m. daily) for an excellent introduction to the park, including aquariums, exhibits, and a video program. Reservations are advisable for glass-bottom boat tours; call (305) 451-1621. Ranger led canoe trips and nature walks are also offered. Concessions rent boats and diving equipment and offer scuba and snorkel boat tours. The loop of the Wild Tamarind Trail begins not far from the visitor center; the Mangrove Trail lies farther to the east. Check these areas for spring migrant birds, black-whiskered vireos (summer), and mangrove cuckoos (summer). *CORAL REEF IS VERY FRAGILE. IT IS ILLEGAL TO COLLECT CORAL OR TROPICAL FISH. USE MOORING BUOYS RATHER THAN ANCHORS.*

**Directions:** *Entrance is off U.S. Highway 1 at Key Largo.*

DeLorme map 122

**Ownership:** Department of Environmental Protection (305) 451-1202
**Size:** 53,000 submerged acres; 2,350 upland acres
**Closest town:** Key Largo

*Concession services at John Pennekamp Coral Reef State Park make it easy for almost everyone to see the colorful reef, either by snorkeling, scuba diving, or glass bottom boat tours.* DOUG PERRINE

SOUTHEAST

**Description:** Visitors to this pristine island—accessible only by private boat—can easily imagine how the Keys must have looked before bridges and commercial development. There are more than sixty-five species of trees and shrubs in the tropical hammock, including gumbo limbo, strangler fig, mahogany, and the small, flowering lignumvitae tree for which the island is named. The hammock attracts many species of butterflies and sustains a protected population of large, colorful, liguus tree snails. A caretaker's residence, the Matheson House, has been restored and turned into a modest visitor center. Look for white-crowned pigeons, brown pelicans, ospreys, double-crested cormorants, gulls, terns, wading birds, and migratory warblers. Black-whiskered vireos and mangrove cuckoos may be seen in summer and fall. All visitors join ranger-led tours of the island Thursday through Monday, 10:00 a.m. and 2:00 p.m.

**Viewing Information:** Private boats must dock at the main dock on the island and join a guided walk, Thursday–Monday at 10:00 a.m. and 2:00 p.m.

*Directions: For tour boat service information, call Robbie's Boat Rentals (305) 664-9814.*

DeLorme map 123

**Ownership:** Department of Environmental Protection (305) 664-2540
**Size:** 280 acres
**Closest town:** Islamorada

*There are at least 58 different color variations of tree snails. It's illegal to disturb or remove these two-inch jewels. Destruction of tropical hardwood hammocks, the snail's habitat, along with overcollecting, threaten these Florida natives.* WILLIAM J. WEBER

**Description:** Every fall, the Florida Keys act as a migratory bottleneck for about 16 species of falcons, hawks, and other raptors en route to southern wintering grounds. Hawk watchers have determined that Boot Key is an especially fine (yet little known) location to spot a wide range of species during migration. In fall 1995, biologists tabulated high numbers of migrating peregrine falcons, second only to counts at Cape May, New Jersey.

**Viewing Information:** The earliest raptors spotted by hawk watchers are usually swallow-tailed kites, in late August and September. Ospreys and Mississippi kites are also early migrants through the Keys. Though the migration often continues into early November, the first week of October is often the most dependable for other species, including broad-winged, Swainson's, and sharp-shinned hawks; American kestrels; and peregrine falcons. Boot Key can also be successfully birded for migratory songbirds during the spring and fall months, as well as mangrove cuckoos and other Keys specialties. Do your observing from the roadside; Boot Key is entirely under private ownership.

*Directions: As you travel south on U.S. Highway 1 through Marathon, turn left (east) on County Road 931 (mile marker 48.1). Stop and scan the cellular phone tower on the left for resting bald eagles and peregrine falcons, especially at dawn and dusk. At the drawbridge, and for the next mile, very productive birding is likely from the roadside; bring a spotting scope as well as binoculars.*

**Ownership:** N/A
**Size:** N/A
**Closest town:** Marathon

The endangered peregrine falcon is still recovering from serious population decline caused by pesticide exposure. Though the falcon doesn't breed in Florida, its impressive speed and power are still visible when it passes through the state on its annual migrations between northern nesting grounds and wintering areas in Central and South America.

JIM ROETZEL

SOUTHEAST

## 125 PIGEON KEY

**Description:** Two main viewing areas are available: the Old Seven Mile Bridge, which spans 2.2 miles of saltwater and sand flats, and the island of Pigeon Key, which is surrounded by crystal clear waters. Seven simple buildings—all on the National Register of Historic Places—imbue the island with the feel of earlier times. Some birders believe that the middle Keys (including Pigeon) are the best under-publicized areas in North America for fall raptor migration.

**Viewing Information:** A leisurely walk across the Old Seven Mile Bridge can allow the visitor to view a good assortment of wading birds, including great white herons, roseate spoonbills, and reddish egrets. Watch for magnificent frigatebirds overhead. Fall raptor migration (late September through early December) can be spectacular, yielding sightings of at least 15 species of hawks, vultures, ospreys, bald eagles, kestrels, merlins, and peregrine falcons. Bottlenose dolphin, tarpon, and various rays are often seen in the deep channels of Florida Bay.

**Directions:** *Access to the site is located at mile marker 48 on U.S. Highway 1, at the west end of Marathon in the Florida Keys. Parking is available at the Pigeon Key Visitor's Center on Knight's Key. A tram service shuttles visitors across the Old Seven Mile Bridge to Pigeon Key; visitors may also walk, bicycle, or skate the 2-mile distance.*

Delorme Map 124

**Ownership:** Monroe County and the Pigeon Key Foundation (305) 289-0025
**Size:** 5 acres
**Closest town:** Marathon

*The reddish egret has a gray body, with rust-colored plumes on its head and neck. It is found primarily in shallow saltwater flats and lagoons, where it employs an unusual feeding method characterized by "dances" or short dashes through shallow water with wings extended.*

TOM VEZO

**Description:** Located just north of Big Pine Key, this park occupies all of Bahia Honda Key. White sand beaches on the Atlantic Ocean and Florida Bay offer some of the best swimming in the Keys. The beaches are backed by an almost impenetrable thicket of lush tropical hardwood forest. Yellow satinwood, gumbo limbo, and silver palm trees may be viewed along the nature trail that follows the shore of a tidal lagoon at the far end of Sandspur Beach. Canoeing through narrow channels in the mangroves surrounding the lagoons provides solitude and birding opportunities. The park is very popular for swimming, snorkeling, and fishing, and is sometimes closed when it reaches capacity.

**Viewing Information:** Park beaches offer year-round viewing of brown pelicans, double-crested cormorants, great blue, little blue, and great white herons, as well as ospreys, laughing gulls, and sanderlings. In winter, additional species such as white ibises, willets, western sandpipers, ring-billed gulls, and common and royal terns are frequently seen. The self-guided Silver Palm Nature Trail provides good interpretation of the tropical hammock and attracts migratory warblers in the spring and fall. Check this area in summer and fall for black-whiskered vireos and mangrove cuckoos, and year-round for smooth-billed anis. White-crowned pigeons may be seen year-round. Guided walks through the nature trail are available, as are daily snorkel trips to the reefs of the Looe Key National Marine Sanctuary.

**Directions:** *The park entrance is at Mile Marker 36.9, off of U.S. Highway 1 on Bahia Honda Key.*

DeLorme map 124

**Ownership:** Department of Environmental Protection (305) 872-2353
**Size:** 635 acres
**Closest town:** Big Pine

*Although relatively uncommon, smooth-billed anis nest on the southern half of the Florida peninsula. A long tail, and large, crested bill distinguish this subtropical species from blackbirds and crows.* JEFF FOOTT

SOUTHEAST

**Description:** Big Pine Key is the largest of the middle keys and the only one with a permanent source of fresh water. This mangrove-fringed island contains extensive areas of stunted pinewoods typical of the Keys, as well as areas of tropical hardwood hammock characterized by gumbo limbo, poisonwood, and many other unusual species. Mudflats are exposed at low tide and provide feeding areas for wading birds, including roseate spoonbills. The diminutive, collie-sized Key deer feed along the edges of the roads.

**Viewing Information:** From U.S. Highway 1, turn north onto County Road 940 (Key Deer Boulevard). The refuge headquarters is in the Big Pine Shopping Center on the right. Go 1.7 miles to Watson Boulevard. Endangered Key deer are most frequently sighted along this road in early evening. *DO NOT FEED DEER.* Blue Hole observation pool is located 1.25 miles farther north on Key Deer Boulevard. From the viewing platform at this old quarry, look for turtles, alligators, and fish. The Jack C. Watson Wildlife Trail interprets local flora and begins 0.25 mile north of Blue Hole on Key Deer Boulevard. The refuge office is open 8:00 a.m. to 5:00 p.m. Monday through Friday; brochures for Blue Hole and Watson trails available. Partial barrier-free access.

**Directions:** *From U.S. Highway 1 on Big Pine Key, turn north onto County Road 940 (Key Deer Boulevard) and follow signs to the sites.*

DeLorme map 124

**Ownership:** U.S. Fish and Wildlife Service (305) 872-2239
**Size:** 8,005 acres
**Closest town:** Big Pine Key

*The tiny Key deer is a distinct subspecies of common white-tailed deer. Two-thirds of the endangered Key deer population of 250-300 animals live on Big Pine Key. To help these deer avoid extinction, obey all speed limits while driving on the Keys, and don't feed them. Feeding attracts deer to roadsides, where dozens are killed each year by automobiles.* JOHN NETHERTON

**Description:** About 70 miles west of Key West in the Gulf of Mexico lies a cluster of seven coral reefs, the Dry Tortugas, known worldwide for its fabulous bird and marine life, and its legends of pirates and sunken gold. The Park also includes the largest of the 19th century American coastal forts.

**Viewing Information:** A spring visit to this park is considered a highlight of a birding trip to Florida. Spring and fall migrations are especially good times to view a terrific assortment of warblers, vireos, and other songbirds. Keep an eye out for West Indian species that have strayed to the Dry Tortugas, including ruddy quail-dove, variegated flycatcher, loggerhead kingbird, Bahama swallow, Bahama mockingbird, thick-billed vireo, and yellow-faced grassquit. Nesting seabirds include magnificent frigatebird, masked booby, sooty tern, and brown noddy, visible primarily on the more inaccessible keys (by boat). Since there is no naturally occurring fresh water on the islands, the birding is limited in the summer and winter months. Snorkeling the coral reefs can be rewarding any month of the year. The islands are open to the public year-round, but are accessible only by seaplane or boat. You can take a day trip by charter boat (8 a.m. to 7 p.m.) to 16-acre Garden Key, where Fort Jefferson is located. Activities on Garden Key include walking and snorkeling.

**Directions:** Call the Key West Chamber of Commerce for information about boat and air taxi service (305) 294-2587 or (800) 648-6269.

DeLorme Map 126

**Ownership:** National Park Service (305) 242-7700
**Size:** 64,700 acres
**Closest town:** Key West

*One of the highlights of a trip to the Dry Tortugas is a glimpse of the masked booby. The masked booby is the largest of the boobies, named for its dark face pattern.*
JEFF FOOTT

SOUTHEAST

# POPULAR WILDLIFE VIEWING SPECIES OF FLORIDA

The index below identifies some of the more interesting, uncommon, or popular species found in Florida, as well as some of the best places to see them. Many of the animals listed may be viewed at other sites as well. The list includes some threatened (T) or endangered species (E).The numbers following each species refer to viewing sites.

# FOR FURTHER READING

*A birder's guide to Florida*
Bill Pranty
American Birding Association, Colorado Springs, 1996

*Florida parks: a guide to camping in nature*
Gerald Grow
Longleaf Publications, Tallahassee, 1989

*The Sierra Club guide to the natural areas of Florida*
John and Jane G. Perry
Sierra Club Books, San Francisco, 1992

*Exploring wild south Florida*
Susan D. Jewell
Pineapple Press, Sarasota, 1993

*Florida nature photography*
William J. Weber
University Press of Florida, Gainesville, 1992

## Organizations in Florida with regular outings and helpful publications:

Florida Trail Association publishes *The Footprint*
3410 W. Trapnell Road
Plant City, Florida 33567

Florida Association of Canoe Liveries and Outfitters publishes *Florida Canews*
PO Box 1764
Arcadia, Florida 33821

Florida Chapter of the Sierra Club publishes *The Pelican*
1112 Riflecrest Ave
Valrico, FL 33594

## Identification guides:

*Florida's Fabulous Reptiles and Amphibians*
Pete Carmichael and Winston Williams
World Publications
Tampa, 1991

*Birds of North America: a guide to field identification*
C.S. Robbins, B. Bruun, and H.S. Zim
Golden Press, New York, 1966

## Helpful (free) Publications:

*Bird Watching Basics: An introduction for beginning bird watchers*

*Florida's Venomous Snakes*

*Florida's Nonvenomous Snakes*

All three titles available from:
Florida Game & Fresh Water Fish Commission
620 South Meridian Street
Tallahassee, FL 32399-1600

*Common Florida natural areas*
Florida Conservation Foundation, Inc.
1191 Orange Avenue
Winter Park, Florida 32789

# Discover the Thrill of Watching Wildlife.

## The Watchable Wildlife® Series

Published in cooperation with Defenders of Wildlife, these high-quality, full color guidebooks feature detailed descriptions, side trips, viewing tips, and easy-to-follow maps. Wildlife viewing guides for the following states are now available with more on the way.

| | | |
|---|---|---|
| Alaska | Massachusetts | Oregon |
| Arizona | Montana | Puerto Rico & |
| California | Nebraska | Virgin Islands |
| Colorado | Nevada | Tennessee |
| Florida | New Hampshire | Texas |
| Idaho | New Jersey | Utah |
| Indiana | New Mexico | Vermont |
| Iowa | New York | Virginia |
| Kentucky | North Carolina | Washington |
| | North Dakota | West Virginia |
| | Ohio | Wisconsin |

*Watch for this sign along roadways. It's the official sign indicating wildlife viewing areas included in the Watchable Wildlife® Series.*

FALCON®

# FALCON GUIDES® Leading the way™

FalconGuides® are available for where-to-go hiking, mountain biking, rock climbing, walking, scenic driving, fishing, rockhounding, paddling, birding, wildlife viewing, and camping. We also have FalconGuides on essential outdoor skills and subjects and field identification. The following titles are currently available, but this list grows every year. For a free catalog with a complete list of titles, call FALCON toll-free at 1-800-582-2665.

## BIRDING GUIDES

Birding Minnesota
Birding Montana
Birding Northern California
Birding Texas
Birding Utah

## ROCKHOUNDING GUIDES

Rockhounding Arizona
Rockhounding California
Rockhounding Colorado
Rockhounding Montana
Rockhounding Nevada
Rockhound's Guide to
   New Mexico
Rockhounding Texas
Rockhounding Utah
Rockhounding Wyoming

## WALKING

Walking Colorado Springs
Walking Denver
Walking Portland
Walking St. Louis
Walking Virginia Beach

## CAMPING GUIDES

Camping California's
   National Forests
Camping Colorado
Camping Southern California
Camping Washington

## ALL FIELD GUIDES

Bitterroot: Montana State Flower
Canyon Country Wildflowers
Central Rocky Mountain
   Wildflowers
Great Lakes Berry Book
New England Berry Book
Ozark Wildflowers
Pacific Northwest Berry Book
Plants of Arizona
Rare Plants of Colorado
Rocky Mountain Berry Book
Scats & Tracks of the Pacific
   Coast States
Scats & Tracks of the Rocky Mtns.
Southern Rocky Mountain
   Wildflowers
Tallgrass Prairie Wildflowers
Western Trees
Wildflowers of Southwestern Utah
Willow Bark and Rosehips

## PADDLING GUIDES

Floater's Guide to Colorado
Paddling Minnesota
Paddling Montana
Paddling Okefenokee
Paddling Oregon
Paddling Yellowstone & Grand
   Teton National Parks

## HOW-TO GUIDES

Avalanche Aware
Backpacking Tips
Bear Aware
Desert Hiking Tips
Hiking with Dogs
Leave No Trace
Mountain Lion Alert
Reading Weather
Route Finding
Using GPS
Wilderness First Aid
Wilderness Survival

## MORE GUIDEBOOKS

Backcountry Horseman's
   Guide to Washington
Camping California's
   National Forests
Exploring Canyonlands & Arches
   National Parks
Exploring Hawaii's Parklands
Exploring Mount Helena
Recreation Guide to WA
   National Forests
Touring California & Nevada
   Hot Springs
Trail Riding Western
   Montana
Wild Country Companion
Wilderness Directory
Wild Montana
Wild Utah

■ *To order any of these books, check with your local bookseller*
*or call FALCON ® at **1-800-582-2665**.*
*Visit us on the world wide web at:*
www.FalconOutdoors.com

**FALCON**GUIDES® Leading the Way™

---

■ *To order any of these books, check with your local bookseller*
*or call FALCON® at **1-800-582-2665**.*
*Visit us on the world wide web at:*
www.FalconOutdoors.com

FALCON®

## FALCON GUIDES® Leading the Way™

■ *To order any of these books, check with your local bookseller
or call FALCON® at **1-800-582-2665**.
Visit us on the world wide web at:
www.FalconOutdoors.com*

FALCON®